Our Heritage in Cross Stitch and Embroidery

Colonial Style cross-stitched Family Tree Sampler

Colonial Style needle-painted Miniature Picture (left), Candlewicked Baby Quilt (right)

Colonial Style embroidered Wildflower Tablecloth

Our Heritage in Cross Stitch and Embroidery

24 Delightful Projects to Make

VIVIENNE GARFORTH

Gold Rush Style Patchwork Quilt Cover and Embroidered Cushions, Jane Opie's Rag Doll

BLITZ EDITIONS

Gold Rush Style cross-stitched Photograph Frame Mounts, cross-stitched Herbal and Potpourri Sachets

Contents

Victorian Style cross-stitched Heart-shaped Potpourri Sachet, cross-stitched Bouquet Bath Towel and Face Washer

Victorian Style Silk-embroidered Greeting Cards, cross-stitched Hearts and Cupids Pillowcases

German Lutheran Style cross-stitched and back-stitched Kitchen Set

German Lutheran Style cross-stitched Wedding Sampler and Ring Pillow

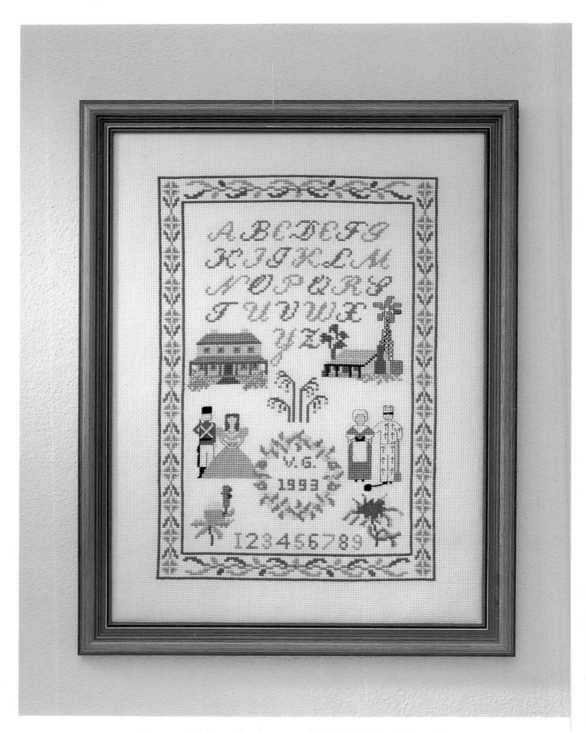

German Lutheran Style cross-stitched Traditional Sampler

German Lutheran Style Berlin Work Cushion

Federation Style Federation House Cross Stitch, embroidered Patchwork Doily

Federation Style embroidered Wildflower Placemats

Federation Style embroidered Apple Blossom Pictures

13

European Influence Whitework Cushion

European Influence Trapunto Quilted Jewellery Roll

European Influence Blackwork Banksia Picture

15

European Influence Cutwork Runner

Introduction

Since the first European settlers arrived in Australia over 200 years ago, very little has been documented about the traditional embroidery styles that have been introduced into our society with the immigration waves which flooded our shores periodically.

Our first embroiderers were the officers' wives and female convicts who landed here, albeit unwillingly, and proceeded to make dogged attempts at home-making with the very limited range of materials on hand and the irregular supplies from England. Most of the sewing and embroidery from the period of European settlement was confined to basic comfort-giving items such as quilts, curtains, cushions and rugs which were well used and, unfortunately, well worn. Some of the work executed skilfully by the wives of the officers was more decorative and therefore kept for posterity. Unfortunately, most of these beautifully embroidered works of art remained hidden in linen cupboards, glory boxes and bottom drawers to be appreciated only by family and close friends.

The style of decorating that developed in Australia from the arrival of the First Fleet until the 1850s was based on the traditions of England, Scotland, Wales and Ireland. It focused on garden and herbal crafts, toy making, embroidery and lace making.

During the gold rush era, however, immigrants fresh from the Californian goldfields arrived, introducing new ideas and methods into the colonies, such as patchwork and folk embroidery.

In 1838 four ships arrived in South Australia carrying German Lutheran immigrants who were seeking refuge from the religious demands of their king and his state church. The women in this group were skilled in embroidery techniques that were centuries old. The cross-stitched samplers, woollen tapestries and colourful peasant-style embroideries they introduced rapidly became popular and were adapted by colonial embroiderers. Meanwhile, migrants were arriving steadily from the United Kingdom, bringing with them all the trappings and clutter of the Victorian era. Australian women picked up the latest embroidery ideas, beaded Berlin work, ribbon embroidery and knotted canvas work, from the new arrivals. During this time differently coloured threads became available. The rich and earthy tones of oranges and reds, greens and blues, purples and yellows against solid backgrounds of black, brown, blue and cream were used to decorate cushions, footstools, pictures, chair backs and all manner of household objects. A great deal of embroidery worked during this period has survived because it was decorative rather than practical.

By 1901, when Australia became a nation of federated states, a new wave of immigrants arrived — they were mostly British but with a growing number of Europeans. With this influx came the pre-hemmed printed linens that had become the vogue for home sewers. The production of tablecloths, doilies, chair backs, pillowcases, tea towels and dressingtable sets was in full swing.

At this time and in the years between the two world wars, the tide of Italian immigrants gained momentum. With the arrival of the new family groups, exquisite embroidery, following the ancient traditions of their local regions, was introduced. White lacework on white linen, colourful silk embroidery and bold black stitching on even-weave fabric reflect the region of origin.

It was the women from these waves of immigration who brought their traditional skills and techniques to a new country and who have inspired the ideas and adaptations in this book, and to whom we owe a great deal of gratitude.

Colonial Style

Family Tree Sampler (photograph on page 1)
Candlewicked Baby Quilt (photograph on page 2)
Miniature Picture (photograph on page 2)
Wildflower Tablecloth (photograph on page 2)

Although there were about 100 female convicts and a few officers' wives aboard the ships of the First Fleet, the first major influx of women into the colony of New South Wales occurred in 1790, when the *Lady Juliana* sailed into Port Jackson carrying 221 convicted females. It was followed shortly afterwards by the remainder of the Second Fleet — bringing part of the newly formed New South Wales Corps and another 76 women convicts.

To ease the enforced idleness brought on by being at sea, each female convict was issued with a parcel of fabric pieces, cotton thread, needle and thimble with which to while away the hours doing constructive needlework. Quilts and mattress covers were sewn in preparation for the difficult and largely unpleasant life that lay ahead.

The wives of the officers and soldiers, however, were much more adept at needlework and most were well equipped with fine materials, embroidery threads, sewing implements and copious supplies of laces, braids and ribbons.

There are some existing examples of the beautifully embroidered articles that had been worked by the more highly skilled and affluent women of the colony; very little remains, however, of the practical sewing, clothing and household necessities done by the female convicts.

The most prolific form of embroidery was probably clothing ornamentation. Such things as baby frocks and bonnets, gentlemen's waistcoats and slippers, ladies' collars, cuffs, bodices and shawls, nightgowns and underwear displayed embroidery skills of one form or another.

It was also important to fill one's home with opulent displays of embroidered cushions, rugs, curtains, chairs, footstools, doilies and tablecloths. The more clutter around the home, the more prestige one received.

Embroidery styles brought to Australia by the first pioneers still form the basis for most of the stitches we use today, although with the invention of machinery much of the intricate handwork has been eliminated.

There are basic needlework stitches and methods which will never change: candlewicking, crewel work, needlepoint or canvas work, surface stitchery and smocking are just as popular now as they were over 200 years ago.

FAMILY TREE SAMPLER

This sampler is an attractive and long-lasting way to display and preserve your family history. It shows the names and dates of one's parents', grandparents' and great grandparents' marriages with the children as the roots on which the tree will continue to grow.

MATERIALS
44 x 55 cm (17⅓ x 21⅔ in) cream 14-count
    Aida fabric
DMC stranded cotton in the following colours:
    3 skeins 400 rust
    1 skein each:
    310 black
    340 purple

435 light brown
444 yellow
543 cream
730 dark green
733 light green
740 orange
838 dark brown
962 bright pink
3716 pale pink

DIRECTIONS

Before doing any work on the embroidery, prepare your graph with the names and marriage dates of your ancestors. To do this, count the number of graph squares in each line and divide this figure by two. This becomes the centre of the lettering block (Figure 1.1). A name such as Annie Hastie, which has 11 letters and a central space making 12 spaces altogether, would be worked with 5 letters and the space on one side of the centre line and the 6 letters on the other.

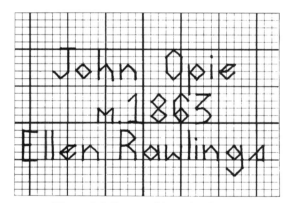

Figure 1.1 Centre of lettering block

Place your lettering blocks onto the graph of the tree, noting if any longer names (such as my sample name, Elizabeth Wooldridge) cross over onto the tree trunk itself. In this case, allow enough room for the name by leaving off some of the squares from the original graph (Figure 1.2).

Prepare the fabric by overlocking the raw edges and then running tacking lines vertically and horizontally through the centre to find the

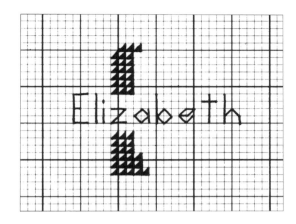

Figure 1.2 Placement of longer names

starting point (Figure 1.3). Working with two strands of cotton, follow the graph in Figure 1.4. Sew the tree trunk first, followed by the leaves. Finish off the cross stitching, then insert the names (Figure 1.5) and dates (Figure 1.6) with two strands of black thread.

When the embroidery is complete, press the work on the wrong side before tightly lacing it over a backing board in preparation for framing (Figures 1.7 and 1.8).

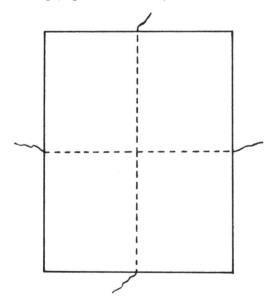

Figure 1.3 Mark the centre with tacking

19

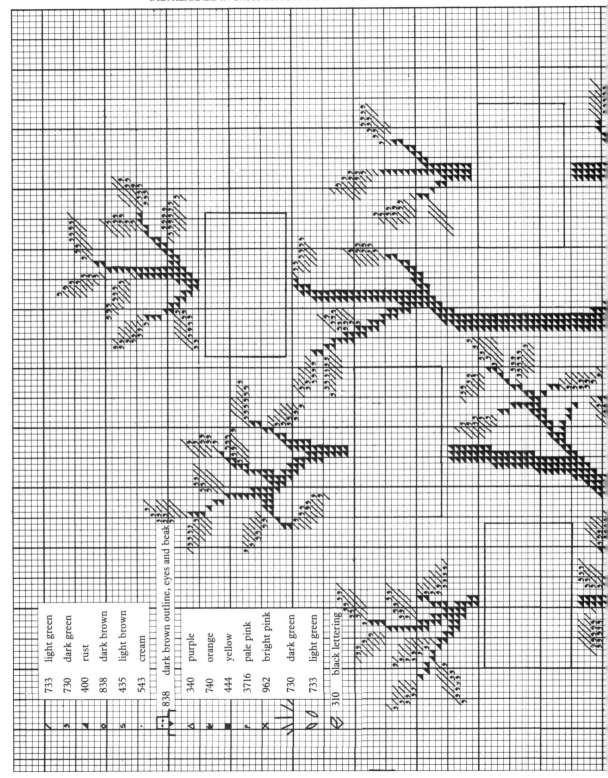

/	733	light green
s	730	dark green
▲	400	rust
◊	838	dark brown
s	435	light brown
·	543	cream
▶	838	dark brown outline, eyes and beak
▲	340	purple
✳	740	orange
■	444	yellow
P	3716	pale pink
✕	962	bright pink
∖	730	dark green
◊	733	light green
◊	310	black lettering

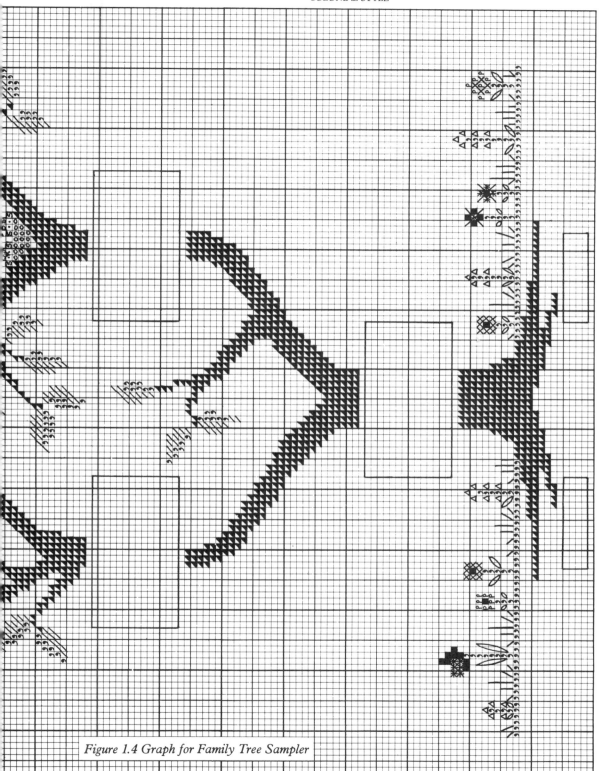

Figure 1.4 Graph for Family Tree Sampler

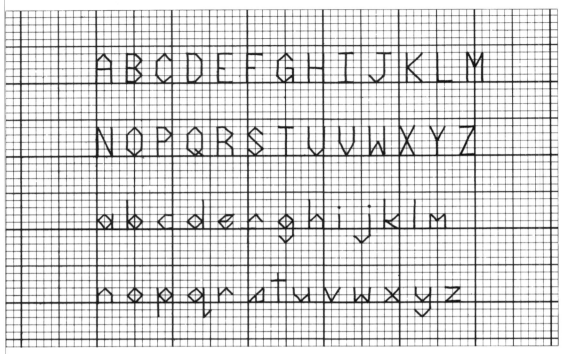

Figure 1.5 Lettering for names

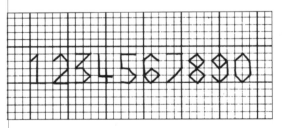

Figure 1.6 Numerals for dates

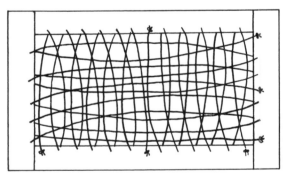

Figure 1.8 Lacing completed

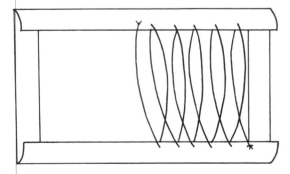

Figure 1.7 Lace the work over a backing board

CANDLEWICKED BABY QUILT

The traditional materials used were unbleached calico and the thick unbleached thread used for making the wicks of candles.

Candlewicking is a decorative and durable embroidery style that is ideal for bedcovers and cushions. With the wide choice of fabrics and threads available today, cleaning candlewicked items is an easy task as it will stand up to regular washing.

This baby quilt has been adapted from the designs used in Australia's convict era, when bed covers were constructed from a single frontpiece and lining, sandwiching several middle layers of fabric between them with stitches taken through all the layers. The animals on the quilt are uniquely Australian and will appeal to young children.

MATERIALS

78 (30¾ in) x 112 cm (1¼ yd) cream fabric such as calico, homespun or twill

3 m (3¼ yd) x 2.5 cm (1 in) broderie anglaise insertion lace

3 m (3¼ yd) x 7 mm (¼ in) cream satin ribbon to fit the holes in the lace

60 cm (23⅔ in) x 1.5 cm (½ in) thick quilt wadding

3 m (3¼ yd) x 6 cm (2⅓ in) gathered broderie anglaise edging lace

Cream candlewicking thread or DMC Cebelia crochet thread

3 m (3¼ yd) x 3 mm (⅛ in) cream satin ribbon

DIRECTIONS

Cut the calico, homespun or twill in half so that it measures 78 x 56 cm (30¾ x 22 in). Prepare the quilt front and back by overlocking the raw edges. Wash in warm water to prevent shrinkage later and leave to dry. Mark out the squares with tacking stitches onto the quilt front. Follow Figure 1.9 for the size of the squares — the centre ones are slightly smaller than the outside ones to allow for the seams.

Thread the ribbon through the eyelet lace,

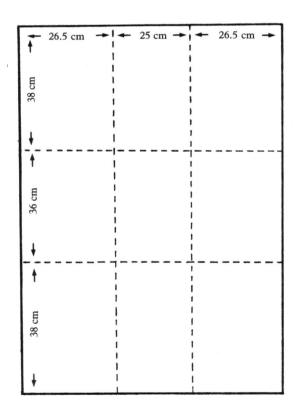

Figure 1.9 Mark the quilt with tacking

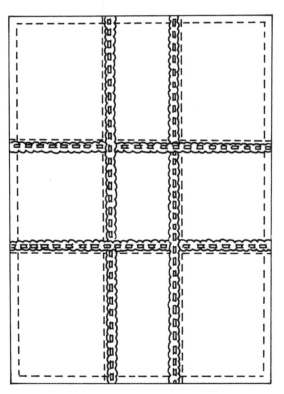

Figure 1.10 Sew lace along internal lines

then cut it into four lengths — two lengths measuring 78 cm (30¾ in) and two lengths measuring 56 cm (22 in).

Sew the longer lengths of lace down and the shorter ones across the internal lines of tacking, laying each length close to the marked line (Figure 1.10).

With a water-soluble or self-fading fabric-marking pen, begin by tracing the design in Figure 1.11 onto the centre square. Work the design with the candlewicking thread before tracing the next pattern. This is necessary if you are using a self-fading pen, as I found that by the time I had completed an animal the ink barely showed at all.

After candlewicking the centre square proceed with the centre top square (Figure 1.12), centre bottom square (Figure 1.13) and then the two centre side squares (Figures 1.14 and 1.15). Finally, work the four corner squares (Figures 1.16, 1.17, 1.18, 1.19). When all the candlewicking has been completed, place a softly padded item, such as a bath towel, on the ironing board and iron the fabric carefully on the wrong side of the work. The fabric is ironed in this manner so that the knots of the candlewicking do not get flattened.

Lay the wadding on the wrong side of the quilt front and place the gathered lace on the right side, matching the raw edge of the lace with the edge of the fabric. Pin through all layers. Join the two raw ends of the lace with tiny hand-sewn stitches so that the stitching is invisible on the right side. Machine sew through all of these layers (Figure 1.20). Lay the backing piece onto the right side of the

Figure 1.12 Bilby design (centre top)

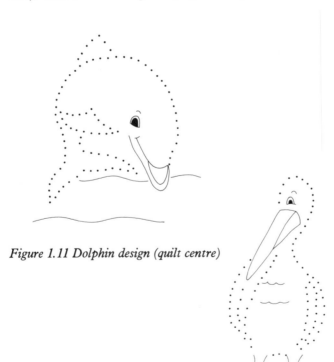

Figure 1.11 Dolphin design (quilt centre)

Figure 1.13 Pelican design (centre bottom)

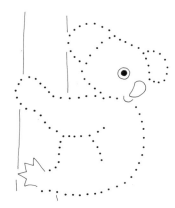

Figure 1.15 Cockatoo design (centre right)

Figure 1.14 Koala design (centre left)

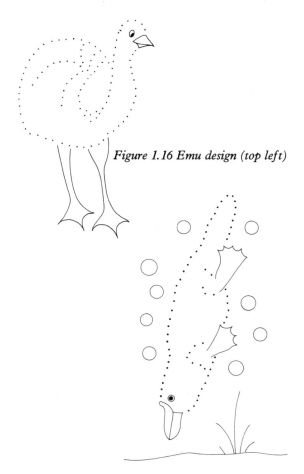

Figure 1.16 Emu design (top left)

Figure 1.17 Sea-lion design (top right)

Figure 1.18 Platypus design (bottom left)

Figure 1.19 Wallaby design (bottom right)

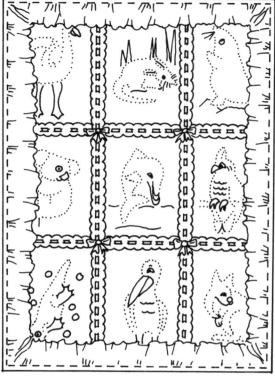
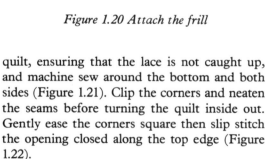

Figure 1.20 Attach the frill

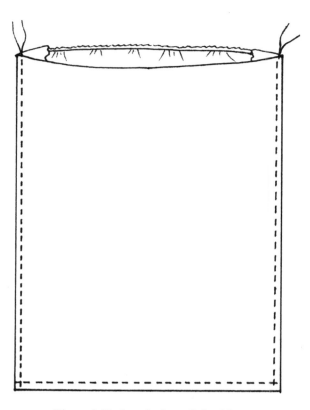

Figure 1.21 Attach the quilt backing

quilt, ensuring that the lace is not caught up, and machine sew around the bottom and both sides (Figure 1.21). Clip the corners and neaten the seams before turning the quilt inside out. Gently ease the corners square then slip stitch the opening closed along the top edge (Figure 1.22).

Cut the 3 m (3¼ yd) length of narrow ribbon into 16 even lengths. Tie into small bows, neatening the raw edges by cutting in a 'V' shape. With strong thread, catch the corners of each square through all layers of fabric and sew three or four tiny tight stitches. On the top of these corner stitches sew a small satin bow. This will create the quilted effect on the completed quilt (Figure 1.23).

MINIATURE PICTURE

The needle-painted scene in this picture is based on an early watercolour of Parramatta painted by George Evans in 1809.

Such early works of art are our only visual records dating from the beginning of European settlement until the invention of photography. Many of the oil and watercolour landscapes depict the vegetation as being vivid greens and golds, similar to the colours of English trees and grasses, while the hills are often shown as the gently rolling slopes of the British Isles. Often the standard of work is naive and amateurish; however, this simply serves to add to the charm and characteristic idealism of these early artists.

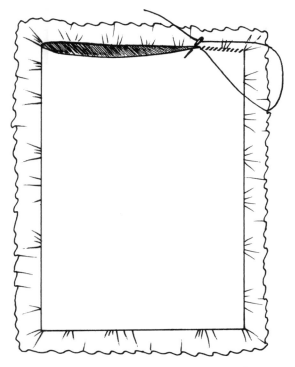

Figure 1.22 Slip stitch to close the top edge

Figure 1.23 Add bows to each corner

MATERIALS

36 x 25 cm (14 x 10 in) heavy-weight cream linen or calico

1 commercial photograph frame with a standard 15 x 10 cm (6 x 4 in) aperture

1 transfer pencil to attach the mirror-image design to the centre of the fabric

1 skein DMC stranded cotton in the following colours:

Sky
827, 828 blues 754, 948 pink streaks

Hills
3041, 3042, 3743 purples, 950 beige

Centre Green Hill
372 fawn, 734 light green

Bushes
502 light green, 3362 dark green

French Knot Bushes
3362 dark green

Fields
422 light fawn, 977 orange

Green fields
472 light green, 732 medium green, 3051 dark green

Houses
310 black for windows (one strand), 712 cream, 3777 dark red

Foreground
301 light rust, 400 deep rust, 632 deep maroon, 833 camel, 977 orange

Water
598 blue, 959 green

Boats
400 rust (small boat), 712 cream (sails), 839 brown (large boat)

DIRECTIONS

When working needle-painting, which is merely row upon row of stem stitches laid next to each other, it is extremely important to watch the tension. If it is too tight, the finished embroidery will be puckered, pulled smaller than the frame and very difficult to flatten. If it is too loose, the stitches will form loops and the end result will not resemble a painted surface.

Before starting the stem stitch, attach the linen background fabric very securely to a slate frame which must be large enough to hold the entire surface (Figure 1.24). Do not stretch a small hoop frame around various areas of the

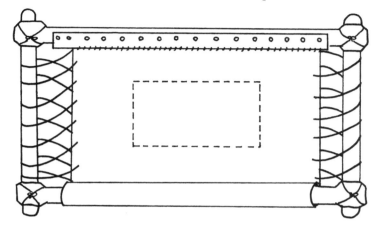

Figure 1.24 Attach the linen securely to a slate frame

Figure 1.25 Design for Miniature Picture

work because the previously sewn areas of the picture will become flattened.

Following Figure 1.25, lay the stitches carefully next to the previous stitch, making sure that the stitch lies flat on the fabric and follows the lines of the design such as the curve of a hill or the horizontal flow of water.

The picture is worked with three strands of cotton and the stitching is predominantly stem stitch, with blanket-stitched bushes, satin-stitched houses and French knots dotted along the small headland. For stitch instructions, see the section on Stitches (page 110).

WILDFLOWER TABLECLOTH

MATERIALS

115 x 115 cm (45⅓ x 45⅓ in) cream linen
5 m (5½ yd) cream crocheted lace
DMC stranded cotton in the colours given as a
  guide. I have not given specific code
  numbers for these as any shade of the
  appropriate colour would be suitable.

DIRECTIONS

Machine stitch a narrow hem around all four sides of the tablecloth, then stitch the lace around the hemmed edges, either gathering or mitring the corners. Neatly hand sew the two ends of the lace edging together. Iron the fabric in half to form a crease along the centre, then repeat in the other direction so that the creases divide the cloth into four sections. Using dressmaker's carbon paper, trace the enlarged

Figure 1.26 Design for Wildflower Tablecloth

design evenly onto each quarter matching flowers so that it forms a continuous circle (Figure 1.26).

Work the flowers using any combination of the stitches suggested in the guide or follow the exact pattern. For stitch instructions, see the section on Stitches (page 110). This project is one which relies on individual choice of colour schemes and stitches to accentuate individual table settings and dining room decorating schemes. Colours and stitch guides are given for the flowers working from the bottom of the pattern to the top.

White blanket stitch flowers
Golden-yellow French knot centres
Green stem stitch stems

Pink long and short stitch bells
Deep pink blanket stitch edges
Dark green lazy daisy leaves
Dark green stem stitch stems

Blue satin stitch petals
Lemon satin stitch centres
Light green satin stitch buds
Light green stem stitch stems

Bright yellow and pale lemon French knot
    flowers
Light brown stem stitch stems
Dark green satin stitch leaves and flower bases

Bright orange blanket stitch larger petals
Deep red blanket stitch centre petals
Light green stem stitch stems

Dark green satin stitch and stem stitch leaves
Light green chain stitch stalk
Mauve satin stitch outer petals

Purple satin stitch inner petals
Golden yellow blanket stitch centre

Pale pink lazy daisy top petals
Medium pink lazy daisy centre petals
Deep pink lazy daisy bottom petals
Grey-green chain stitch stalks
Grey-green straight stitch grass

Golden yellow blanket stitch flowers
Burgundy long and short stitch centres,
    worked into a central point to form an open
    hole
Pale green stem stitch stems
Pale green lazy daisy leaves

Apricot satin stitch petals
Yellow satin stitch centres
Fawn stems
Dark green straight stitch leaves

Light green stem stitch stems
Light green lazy daisy leaves
Pale blue lazy daisy flowers
Bright orange French knot centres
Dark green satin stitch lower leaves

Bright yellow long and short stitch petals
Lime green long and short stitch centres
Light orange French knot or colonial knot
    pollen
Light green stems and grass

Deep muted mauve chain stitch petals on
    upper flower
Pale muted mauve chain stitch petals on lower
    flowers
Apricot blanket stitch centres
Medium green stem stitch stems
Dark green satin stitch leaves

Gold Rush Style

Patchwork Quilt Cover and Embroidered Cushions
(photograph on page 3)
Herbal and Potpourri Sachets (photograph on page 4)
Jane Opie's Rag Doll (photograph on page 3)
Photograph Frame Mounts (photograph on page 4)

With the discovery of gold in Australia in 1846, immigration escalated with many of the new settlers coming from North America, China, South Africa and Europe. Many of these new arrivals were not single men intent on finding a fortune on the diggings but families who settled in the goldfield towns and remained long after the disillusioned prospectors had drifted away.

The American women introduced embroidery styles with a strong Scandinavian influence: solid colour patchwork and bright simplistic folk embroidery. Hours of time and effort went into every small embroidered labour of love — monogrammed handkerchiefs; handworked bed sheets, pillows and quilts; curtains and cushions; and delicate baby clothes were a source of pride and a permanent display of the embroiderer's skill with a needle.

PATCHWORK QUILT COVER AND CUSHIONS

Quilt Cover

MATERIALS

70 cm (27½ in) x 115 cm (1¼ yd) six different printed cotton fabrics for the square patches
25 cm (10 in) extra patterned fabric for the edges of the quilt cover
2.25 x 1.5 m (2½ x 1⅔ yd) plain cotton backing fabric
Large press-stud fasteners to close the cover

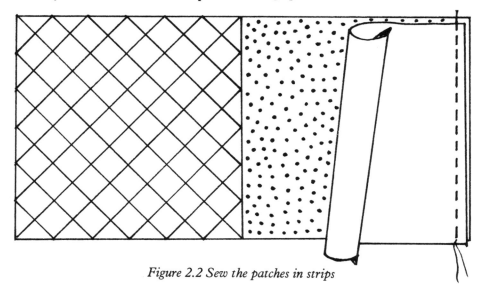

Figure 2.2 Sew the patches in strips

1	2	3	4	5	6	1	2	3	4	5	6
2	3	4	5	6	1	2	3	4	5	6	1
3	4	5	6	1	2	3	4	5	6	1	2
4	5	6	1	2	3	4	5	6	1	2	3
5	6	1	2	3	4	5	6	1	2	3	4
6	1	2	3	4	5	6	1	2	3	4	5
1	2	3	4	5	6	1	2	3	4	5	6
2	3	4	5	6	1	2	3	4	5	6	1
3	4	5	6	1	2	3	4	5	6	1	2
4	5	6	1	2	3	4	5	6	1	2	3
5	6	1	2	3	4	5	6	1	2	3	4
6	1	2	3	4	5	6	1	2	3	4	5
1	2	3	4	5	6	1	2	3	4	5	6
2	3	4	5	6	1	2	3	4	5	6	1
3	4	5	6	1	2	3	4	5	6	1	2
4	5	6	1	2	3	4	5	6	1	2	3
5	6	1	2	3	4	5	6	1	2	3	4
6	1	2	3	4	5	6	1	2	3	4	5
1	2	3	4	5	6	1	2	3	4	5	6
2	3	4	5	6	1	2	3	4	5	6	1

Figure 2.1 Diagram for placing quilt cover patchwork pieces

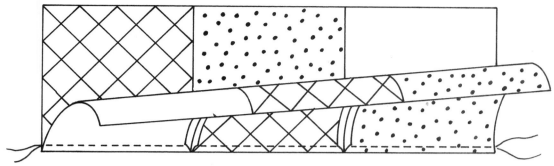

Figure 2.3 Sew the strips together

DIRECTIONS

Cut the six pieces of printed fabric into 13 cm (5⅛ in) squares. Following Figure 2.1, place the pieces in a horizontal pattern. Sew them together in strips of twelve patches across the width of the quilt cover (Figures 2.2 and 2.3).

When all the piecing is finished, press open all the seams on the back of the work, then cut the extra 25 cm (10 in) of fabric into four lengths. Join two of these across the centre and

press out flat. Repeat with the other two lengths. Sew these lengths of fabric down the sides of the patchwork (Figure 2.4).

Lay the backing piece face down onto the quilt top and sew around the top and both sides (Figure 2.5). Turn the quilt cover inside out and gently pull out the corners to make them square. Turn under a 3 cm (1¼ in) hem around the top edge. From the outside edge, sew the opening closed for a distance of 25 cm (10 in) on both

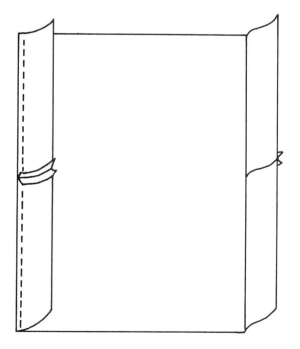

Figure 2.4 Join side pieces to quilt

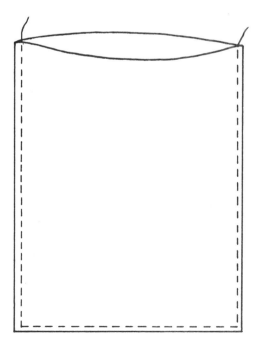

Figure 2.5 Join quilt backing to front

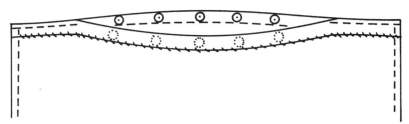

Figure 2.6 Hem quilt opening and add fasteners

sides. Sew the press-stud fasteners across the opening, insert the continental quilt and snap the quilt cover closed (Figure 2.6).

Cushions

MATERIALS

80 x 120 cm (31½ x 47¼ in) calico
80 x 120 cm (31½ x 47¼ in) thin quilt wadding
9 skeins DMC stranded cotton — 815 burgundy
65 cm (25½ in) x 120 cm (1¼ yd) printed cotton fabric for frill
2 bags polyester cushion filling for each cushion
Cream sewing machine thread

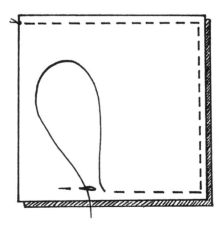

Figure 2.7 Tack calico square to wadding square

DIRECTIONS

Cut the calico and the thin quilt wadding into six 40 cm (15¾ in) squares.

Tack one square of calico and one square of quilt wadding together around the edges (Figure 2.7). The wadding will give the fabric extra body while the heavy embroidery is being completed.

Using a transfer pencil, trace the enlarged design (Figures 2.8 and 2.9) for each cushion onto tissue paper, then iron it onto the cushion front. Using three strands of stranded cotton throughout, work the embroidery using a variety of stitches — stem stitch, blanket stitch, satin stitch, French knots and chain stitch. For stitch instructions, see the section on Stitches (page 110). These pictures lend themselves to being embroidered in a freestyle manner, so while one person may prefer an open area, another individual may fill it in with satin stitches. In this case, the method of stitch combination is left to choice.

When the embroidery is completed, iron on the wrong side of the cushion front, then tack a piece of wadding to the backing piece.

Cut the printed fabric into two even 120 cm (47¼ in) lengths — one length for each cushion (Figure 2.10). Cut each length of printed fabric again into three this time (Figure 2.11), and join the three narrow pieces together to form a continuous piece. With a moderate iron, press this frill in half widthwise (Figure 2.12).

Gather around the top of the frill, adding more fullness at the corners, and pin it in place around the edge of the cushion front. Machine

Each square equals 1 cm

Figure 2.8 Design for patchwork cushion (1)

stitch the frill around all four sides (Figure 2.13). Place the backing piece — calico side down — onto the top of the frill and machine sew around the bottom and sides, ensuring that the frill is not caught up and leaving the top open (Figure 2.14). Turn right side out, gently pull out the corners to make them square and fill the cushion with polyester filling.

Slipstitch the bottom of each cushion closed (Figure 2.15).

35

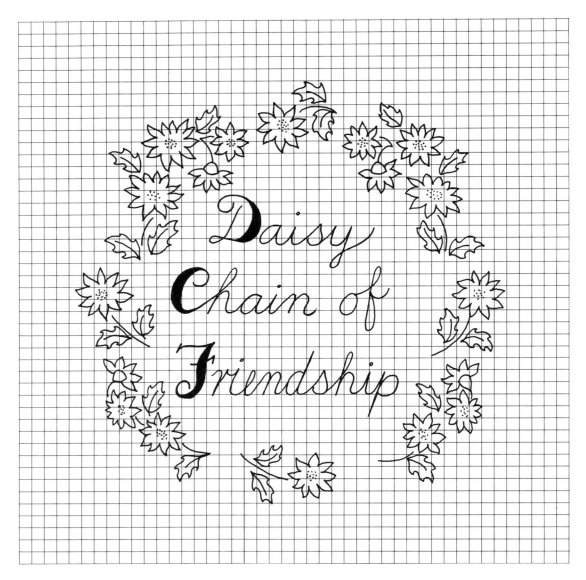

Each square equals 1 cm

Figure 2.9 Design for patchwork cushion (2)

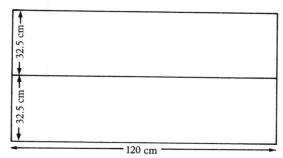

Figure 2.10 Cut frill fabric into two equal lengths

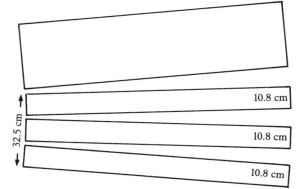

Figure 2.11 Cut each frill length again, into three pieces

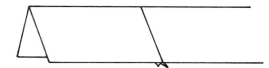

Figure 2.12 Fold and press frill length

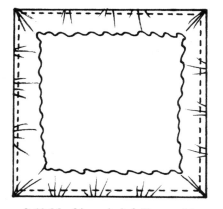

Figure 2.13 Machine stitch frill to cushion cover

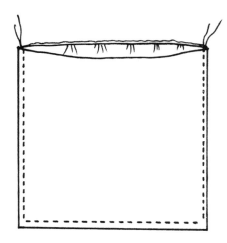

Figure 2.14 Join cushion front to backing, leaving top open

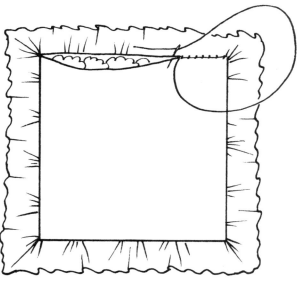

Figure 2.15 Slip stitch to close the filled cushion

HERBAL AND POTPOURRI SACHETS

Herbs and flowers, such as those used in these sachets, were grown for medicinal and culinary use during the gold rush period.

MATERIALS

25 x 70 cm (10 x 27½ in) natural coloured
    14-count Aida cloth
60 cm (22 in) x 1 cm (⅓ in) cream ribbon
Rose, lavender, chamomile, wormwood,
    peppermint, spearmint and rosemary
    potpourris to fill the cushions
DMC stranded cottons in the following
    colours:
    221 rust
    223 dusty pink
    224 pink
    310 black
    333 dark purple
    341 mauve
    580 leaf green
    581 light green
    726 yellow
    732 olive green
    839 brown
    935 dark green
    3023 grey-green
    3746 purple
    3750 dark blue
    white
3 m (3¼ yd) x 5 mm (³⁄₁₆ in) soft rope
3 m (3¼ yd) narrow string or cord
Cream sewing machine thread
Dried herbs to decorate
1 gold ring 3 cm (1¼ in) in diameter.

DIRECTIONS

Cut the Aida cloth into four pieces measuring 16 x 12 cm (4¾ x 6⅓ in) and eight pieces measuring 11.5 x 9 cm (4½ x 3½ in).

Work the cross stitch within the panels indicated in Figures 2.16 and 2.17. Embroider the Moth Repellent and Room Freshener

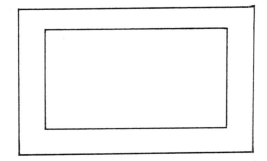

Figure 2.16 Placement of cross stitch on larger sachets

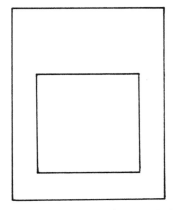

Figure 2.17 Placement of cross stitch on smaller sachets

motifs (Figures 2.18 and 2.19) on two of the larger pieces of Aida cloth. When this is completed, pin the cross-stitched front pieces to their backs.

Sew around the sides and bottom of the two sachets (Figure 2.20) and turn right side out. Fill with potpourri (a rose and lavender combination for the Room Freshener; and chamomile, wormwood, mint and rosemary for the Insect Repellent), cut the cream ribbon in half and insert one end into each top corner of the sachets, and slip stitch them closed (Figure 2.21).

Cross stitch the Roses, Lavender, Chamomile and Peppermint designs onto the four smaller pieces of Aida cloth (Figures 2.22, 2.23, 2.24, 2.25). When completed, sew along the sides and the bottom of each sachet and pull out three threads along the top to form a small

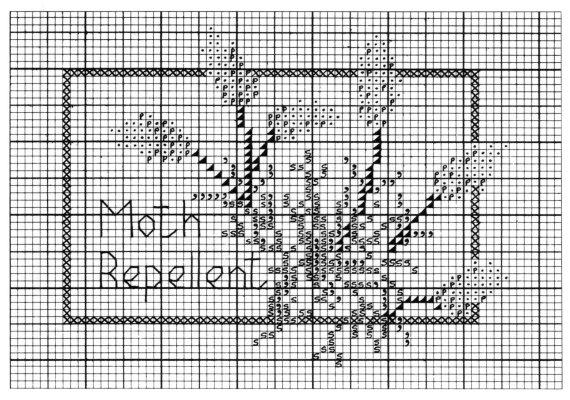

Figure 2.18 Graph of Moth Repellent motif

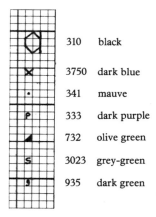

	310	black
	3750	dark blue
	341	mauve
P	333	dark purple
	732	olive green
s	3023	grey-green
ɟ	935	dark green

fringe (Figure 2.26). Turn sachets inside out.

Fill each sachet with a small quantity of the appropriate potpourri mixture and tie string or cord securely at the top to make a bag shape (Figure 2.27).

Cut the rope into one 2 m (2¼ yd) length and one 1 m (1¹⁄₁₀ yd) length. Fold the 2 m (2¼ yd) length through the gold ring and make the ends even. Lay the 1 m (1¹⁄₁₀ yd) length with the others and wrap the top tightly with the string or cord (Figure 2.28).

Plait the rope down to the bottom 7 cm (2¾ in) and tie again with the string. Stitch the four small bags along the plait, spacing them evenly. Then tie a piece of string around the rope and the top of each bag. Tie a bunch of dried herbs, including two or three cinnamon sticks which will add fragrance and weight, at the bottom of the rope. A smaller bunch of herbs and cinnamon sticks can be used to decorate the top of the rope as well.

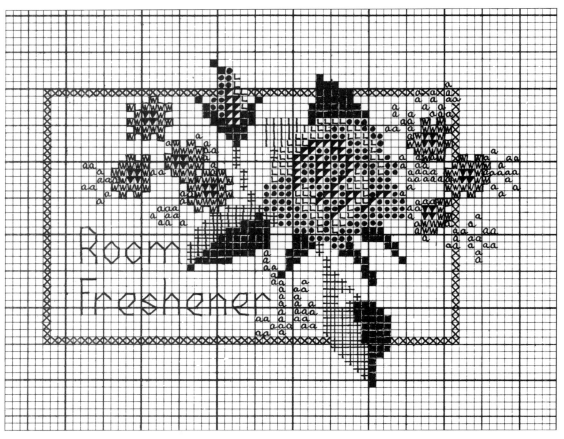

Figure 2.19 Graph of Room Freshener

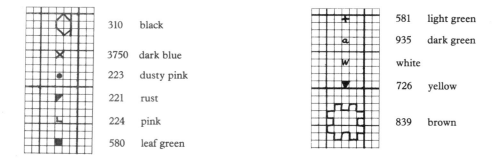

310	black	
3750	dark blue	
223	dusty pink	
221	rust	
224	pink	
580	leaf green	

581	light green	
935	dark green	
	white	
726	yellow	
839	brown	

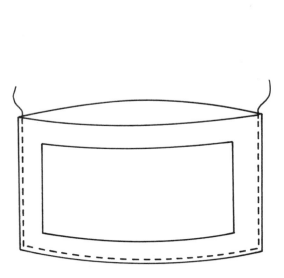

Figure 2.20 Sew back and front of larger sachet

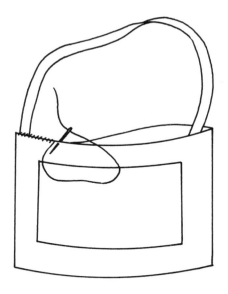

Figure 2.21 Slip stitch ribbon in place and close larger sachet

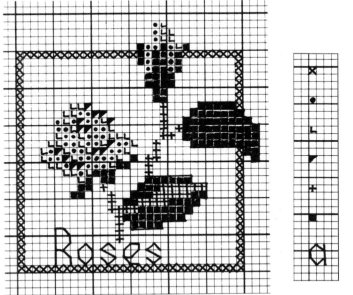

Figure 2.22 Graph for Roses motif

✕	3750	dark blue
●	223	dusty pink
L	224	pink
◢	221	rust
+	581	light green
■	580	leaf green
⬡	310	black

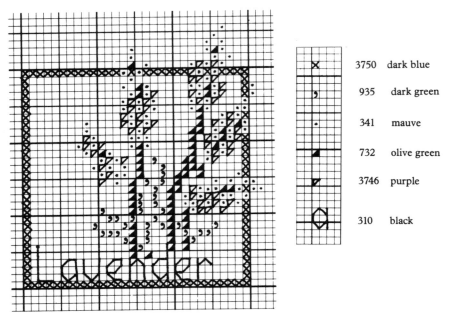

✕	3750	dark blue
,	935	dark green
•	341	mauve
◢	732	olive green
◮	3746	purple
Ɑ	310	black

Figure 2.23 Graph for Lavender motif

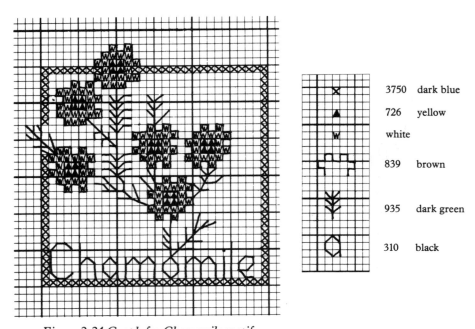

✕	3750	dark blue
▲	726	yellow
W		white
⊓	839	brown
⅄	935	dark green
Ɑ	310	black

Figure 2.24 Graph for Chamomile motif

42

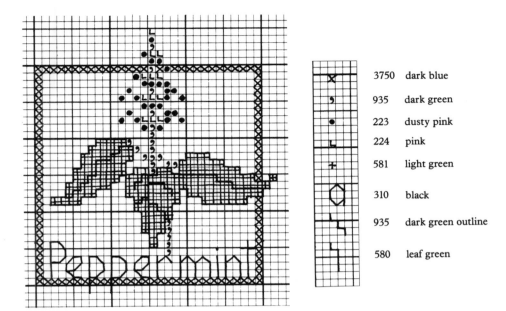

Figure 2.25 Graph for Peppermint motif

X	3750	dark blue
'	935	dark green
•	223	dusty pink
L	224	pink
+	581	light green
◯	310	black
	935	dark green outline
	580	leaf green

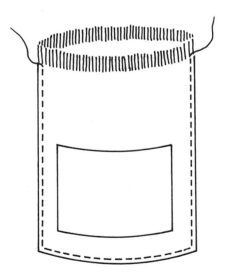

Figure 2.26 Fringe top of smaller sachet

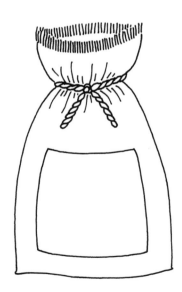

Figure 2.27 Tie up the neck of the smaller sachet

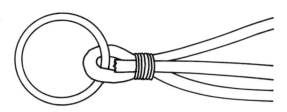

Figure 2.28 Fasten the 1 m and doubled 2 m rope lengths before plaiting

JANE OPIE'S RAG DOLL

In the past parents spent many hours secretly making homemade toys for special occasions such as birthdays and Christmas. Rag dolls were a popular gift and were made from old stockings filled with straw and dressed with left-over scraps of fabric.

This rag doll will delight any small child. The design is based on a traditional rag doll owned by Jane Opie who lived in Ballarat during the gold rush years of the 1860s.

MATERIALS

25 cm (10 in) cream 14-count Aida cloth
50 cm (19¾ in) cream calico for the pinafore and pantaloons
50 cm (19¾ in) printed cotton fabric for the dress and bonnet
70 cm (27½ in) x 1.5 cm (¾ in) cream broderie anglaise edging lace for the pantaloons and pinafore
1 ball 8 ply wool for the wig
Polyester filling for the stuffing
12 cm (4¾ in) black cotton fabric for the boots
DMC stranded cotton in colours to match the dress fabric
DMC stranded cotton in the following colours for the face:
    Eyebrows 420 light brown
    Eyes 798 cornflower blue
    Eyelashes and outline 939 midnight blue
    Nose 352 deep flesh pink
    Cheeks 754 flesh pink
    Lips 3328 dusty rose
    Lip outline and centre 221 maroon

65 cm (25½ in) cream bias binding
1 press-stud fastening
1 cream button
25 cm (10 in) x 3 mm (⅛ in) elastic
Sewing machine cotton in cream, black and a colour to match the printed fabric for the dress

DIRECTIONS

Using the diagrams in Figure 2.29, enlarge all of the pattern pieces to twice the size and cut out the shapes from the appropriate fabrics.

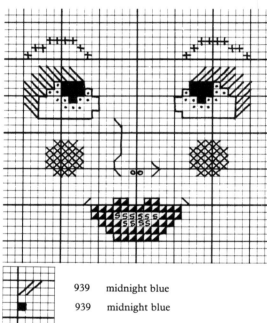

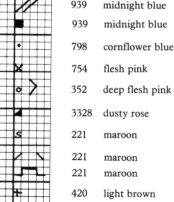

	939	midnight blue
	939	midnight blue
	798	cornflower blue
	754	flesh pink
	352	deep flesh pink
	3328	dusty rose
	221	maroon
	221	maroon
	221	maroon
	420	light brown

Figure 2.30 Graph for rag doll's cross stitched face

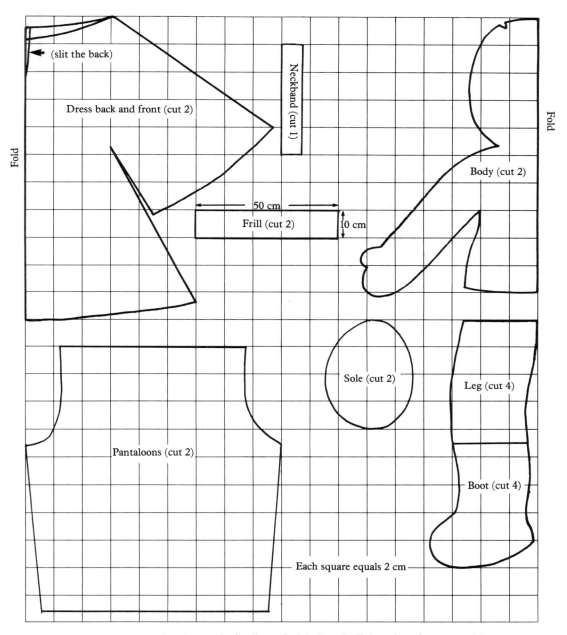

(slit the back)

Dress back and front (cut 2)

Neckband (cut 1)

Fold

Fold

Body (cut 2)

50 cm

Frill (cut 2)

10 cm

Sole (cut 2)

Leg (cut 4)

Pantaloons (cut 2)

Boot (cut 4)

Each square equals 2 cm

Figure 2.29 Cutting guide for Jane Opie's Rag Doll (continued on page 46)

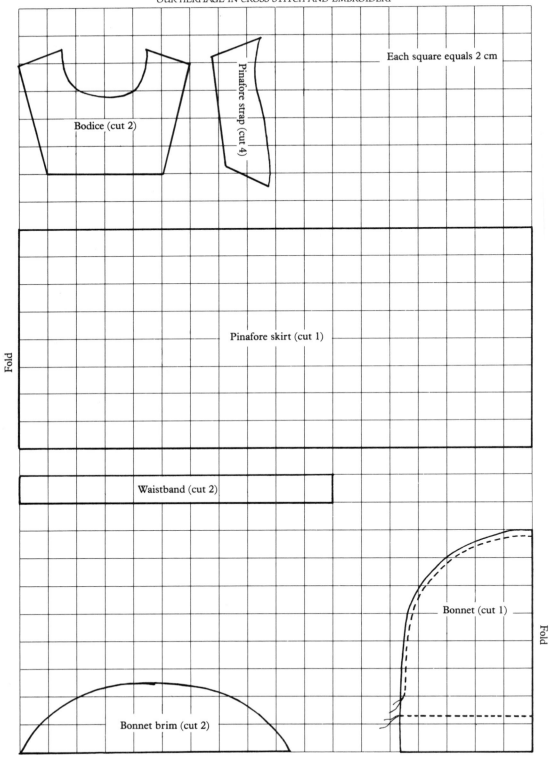

Each square equals 2 cm

Bodice (cut 2)

Pinafore strap (cut 4)

Fold

Pinafore skirt (cut 1)

Waistband (cut 2)

Bonnet (cut 1)

Fold

Bonnet brim (cut 2)

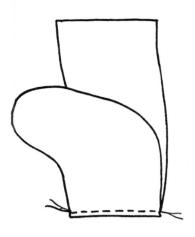

Figure 2.31 Sew boot onto leg

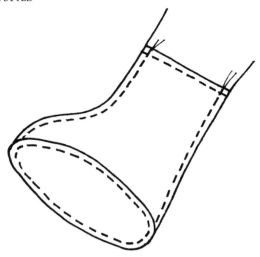

Figure 2.33 Insert boot sole

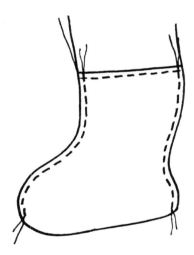

Figure 2.32 Join both halves of boot

Figure 2.34 Join both halves of leg

The Body

1 Embroider the cross-stitched facial features on the Aida cloth (Figure 2.30).
2 Sew the boots onto the ends of the four leg pieces with black cotton (Figure 2.31).
3 Sew the sides of the boots together with black cotton ensuring that right sides are facing (Figure 2.32). Insert the boot sole into the bottom of the foot with black cotton (Figure 2.33). Sew legs together with cream cotton (Figure 2.34). Clip curves and turn inside out.

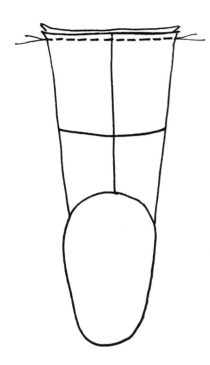

Figure 2.35 Flatten and stitch the stuffed leg

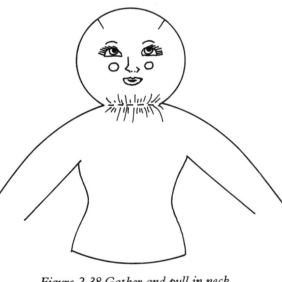

Figure 2.36 Top half body seams, with curves and underarms clipped

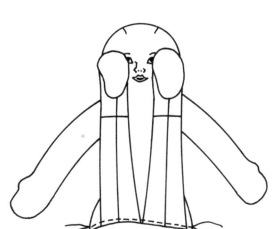

Figure 2.37 Join legs to body front before stuffing top half of body

Figure 2.38 Gather and pull in neck

4 Stuff the legs and feet firmly. Flatten across the top and stitch the top of each leg (Figure 2.35).

5 Sew darts on top of both head pieces.

6 Sew around the head and top half of body and clip the seams around the curves and under the arms (Figure 2.36).

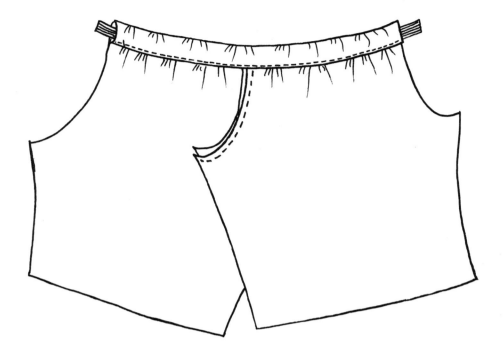

Figure 2.39 Stitch elastic to pantaloons waist

7 Sew legs onto the bottom of the body front, stuff the body and slipstitch the opening closed (Figure 2.37).
8 Gather around the neck and pull in slightly (Figure 2.38).

The Pantaloons

1 Sew down the centre front seam of the two pantaloon pieces.
2 Turn over the hem at the waist, insert 20 cm (7¾ in) of the elastic and stitch it to the waist (Figure 2.39).
3 Turn up a small hem on the bottom of both legs, then stitch two rows of lace across the hems.
4 Sew down the centre back seam.
5 Sew up one leg and down the other, returning with a zigzag stitch to overlock the raw edges.

The Dress

1 With right sides together, sew along shoulder seams.
2 Open the dress out and sew a small hem down the back opening.
3 Turn up a single fold hem across the bottom of the sleeves and zigzag elastic across — approximately 12.5 cm (5 in) for each sleeve.
4 Gather the neck edge. Fold the neckband in half and sew at each end. Sew onto gathered neck edge.
5 Sew up both side seams and down each sleeve, clipping the points at the armholes.
6 Fold the length of frill in half and press with a moderate iron. Gather the frill and sew along the bottom of the dress.
7 Hand sew a press-stud at the back of the neck closing (Figure 2.40).

The Pinafore

1 Sew lace along the bottom of the pinafore, turn it down and stitch along the edge (Figure 2.41).

2 Sew a tiny tuck 2 cm (¾ in) from the stitching line. Hem both back edges of the pinafore skirt.

3 Join the pinafore straps to the bodice at the shoulder seams.

4 Sew the gathered lace frill along the sides of one bodice piece.

5 Lay the other bodice piece face down onto the first piece, ensuring that the lace is pressed towards the centre, and stitch along both sides (Figure 2.42).

6 Turn inside out and stitch close to the edges.

7 With right sides together, sew 30 cm of the bias binding to the neck edge. Slip stitch the binding to the back of the bodice.

Figure 2.40 Back view of dress

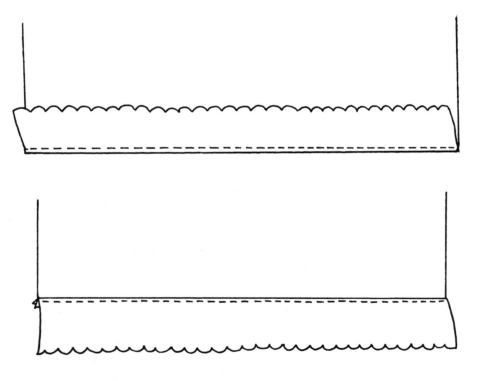

Figure 2.41 Stitch lace to pinafore bottom, then turn and stitch again

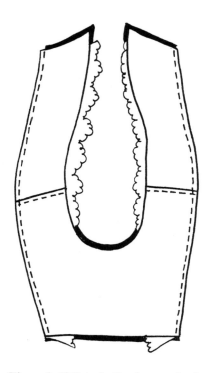

Figure 2.42 Join bodice front to back, sandwiching gathered frill

8 Sew both waistband strips together with the bodice front and back pinned in the correct position (Figure 2.43).

9 Gather the pinafore skirt and sew it to the front waistband strip.

10 Fold over the back waistband strip and slip stitch in place.

11 Sew the grub roses, French knots and lazy daisy leaves (Figure 2.44) onto the bodice and skirt of the pinafore, spacing them 5 cm (2 in) apart.

12 Stitch a cream button to the back left-hand side of the waistband and sew a loop onto the right-hand side.

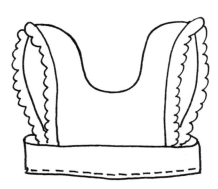

Figure 2.43 Sew waistband to bodice

  Grub rose — two shades of pink

  Lazy daisy leaf — green

  French knots — light colour

  French knots — dark colour

Figure 2.44 Design for grub roses, French knots and lazy daisy leaves

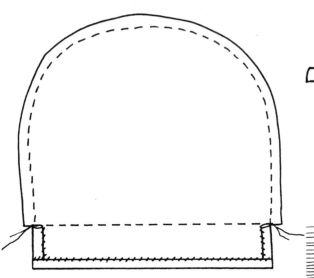

Figure 2.45 Hem sides and bottom of bonnet base

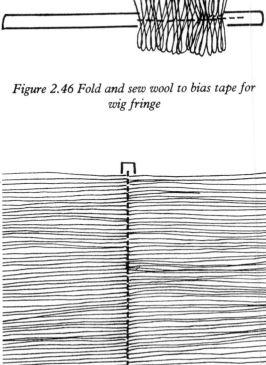

Figure 2.46 Fold and sew wool to bias tape for wig fringe

Figure 2.47 Sew centre of wig to bias tape

The Bonnet

1 With wrong sides together, sew around the curved side of the two brim pieces.
2 Turn the brim inside out and sew close to the curved edge.
3 Where the gathering line is indicated at the base of the bonnet, snip to the seam line. Sew a narrow hem down the two sides and along the straight bottom edge (see Figure 2.45)
4 Sew gathering stitches around the curved shape, then gather in until it fits the raw edge of the brim.
5 Join the two pieces together and neaten the seam.
6 Gather along the straight bottom edge to form a frill.

The Wig

1 To make the fringe, cut a length of bias binding 20 cm (7¾ in) long and fold the wool over approximately 2 cm (¾ in) on each side of the centre. Sew the wool in place as you fold it along the tape (Figure 2.46).

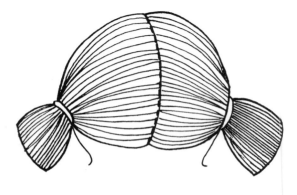

Figure 2.48 Tie pigtails to each side of doll's head

2 Cut another piece of bias binding approximately 15 cm (6 in) long. Cut the remaining wool into lengths of about 36 cm (14 in) long and stitch it along the centre of this piece of tape (Figure 2.47).

3 Using cotton that matches the wig, sew the fringe around the front of the head and the rest of the wig down the back of the head from the fringe to the nape of the neck.

4 Pull the wool hair to the sides of the head in pigtails and tie to the side of the face. Stitch in place (Figure 2.48).

5 Fill the body of the bonnet with extra stuffing and sew it onto the head at the sides and around the back of the neck.

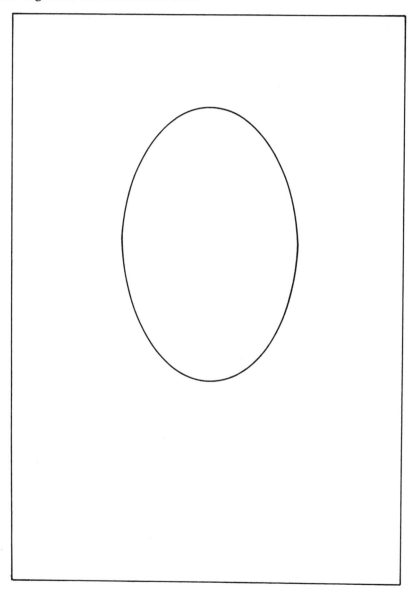

Figure 2.49 Placement of small mount aperture (actual size)

PHOTOGRAPH FRAME MOUNTS

The Small Frame

MATERIALS

30 x 20 cm (11¾ x 7¾ in) cream 14-count
    Aida cloth
1 commercial 15 x 10 cm (6 x 4 in) photograph
    frame kit
15 x 10 cm (6 x 4 in) white cardboard
Craft glue
DMC stranded cotton in the following colours:
    223 dusty pink
    225 pale pink
    730 dark green
    732 olive green
    734 light green
    832 light tan
    3078 pale yellow

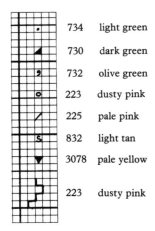

•	734	light green
◀	730	dark green
୨	732	olive green
o	223	dusty pink
/	225	pale pink
S	832	light tan
▼	3078	pale yellow
⌐	223	dusty pink

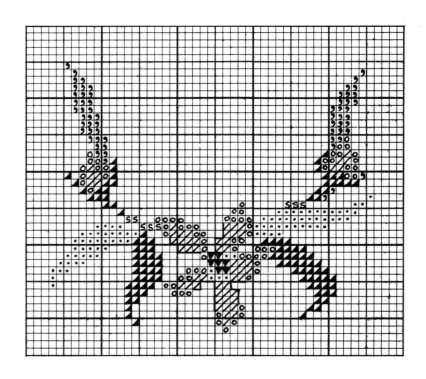

Figure 2.50 Graph for Small Photograph Frame Mount

54

DIRECTIONS

Cut the oval out of the cardboard template (Figure 2.49). Using tacking stitches, mark the outlines of the cardboard template onto the Aida cloth. Work the embroidery in the centre of the lower half following the graph in Figure 2.50.

Place the cardboard template on the wrong side of the cross-stitched fabric and trim the fabric edges back to 1.5 cm (½ in) from the template. Clip away the excess fabric on the corners.

Cut the fabric from inside the oval shape marked on it, keeping within 1.5 cm (½ in) of the tacking stitches outline. Clip this turning edge back to the cardboard edge, fold all turnings over to the wrong side of the cardboard mount and glue in place securely (Figure 2.51).

Make up the frame according to the instructions given on the kit.

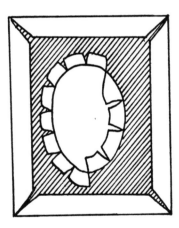

Figure 2.51 Turn and glue clipped fabric edges to back of template

The Large Frame
MATERIALS

35 x 30 cm (13¾ x 11¾ in) cream 14-count Aida cloth
1 commercial 25.5 x 20.5 cm (10 x 8 in) photograph frame kit
25.5 x 20.5 cm (10 x 8 in) white cardboard
Craft glue
DMC stranded cotton in the following colours:
    223 dusty pink
    225 pale pink
    730 dark green
    734 light green
    832 light tan
    3078 pale yellow

DIRECTIONS

Cut the oval out of the centre of the cardboard template (Figure 2.52). With tacking stitches, mark the position of the cardboard template onto the Aida cloth.

Following the graph in Figure 2.53, work the cross-stitched motifs onto the bottom left-hand corner and top right-hand corner of the fabric, then press on the wrong side.

Lay the cardboard onto the wrong side of the work and trim the excess fabric back to 1.5 cm (½ in). Trim excess fabric from corners.

Construct the large frame according to the directions for the small frame.

Make up the frame according to the instructions given with the kit.

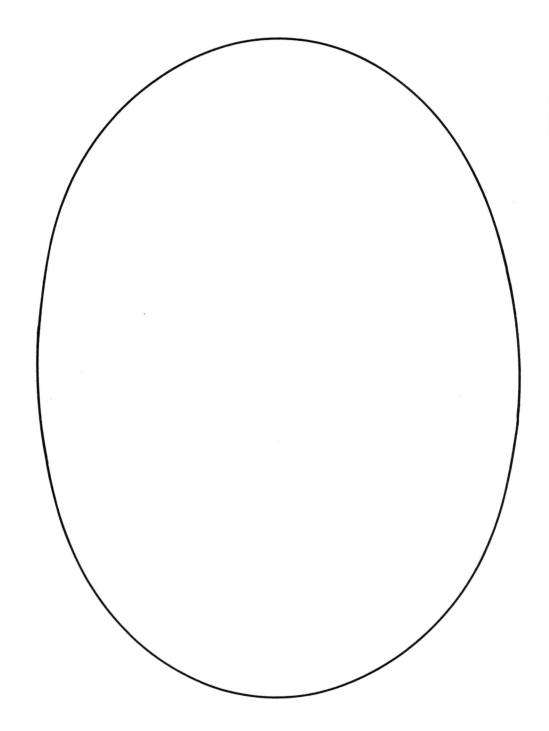

Figure 2.52 Aperture of larger mount (actual size)

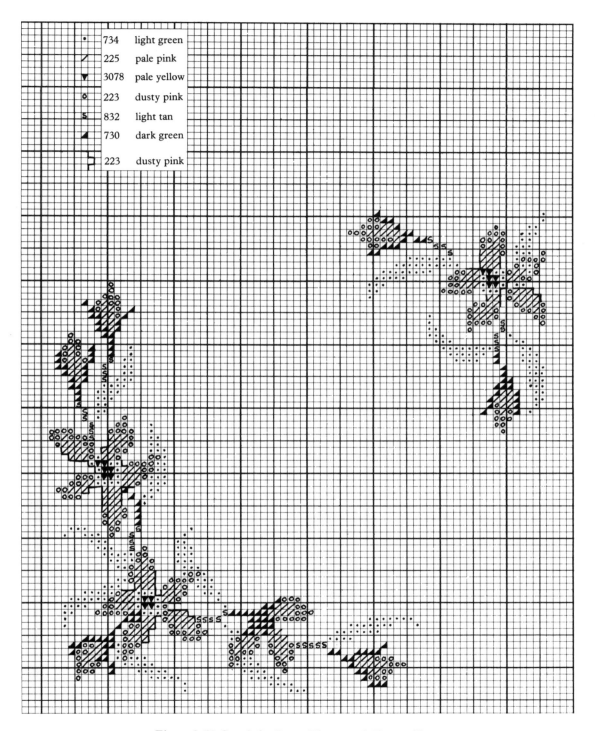

Figure 2.53 Graph for Large Photograph Frame Mount

Victorian Style

Bouquet Bath Towel and Face Washer (photograph on page 6)
Heart-shaped Potpourri Sachet (photograph on page 6)
Silk-embroidered Greeting Cards (photograph on page 7)
Hearts and Cupids Pillowcases (photograph on page 7)

The Victorian era was a time of great change for embroidery throughout the British Isles and Europe. New machinery was being invented to perform tasks that had previously been done by hand. Silk threads, ribbons, braids and lace were made quickly and inexpensively by machine, giving the Victorian embroiderer greater scope to be more creative with threads and fabrics. Synthetic dyes were introduced and needlepoint wools, cotton embroidery threads, metallic braids and yarns, and silks were available in many new colours.

Victorian embroidery was decorative rather than practical and included work with velour threads on velvet, glass beads used with coloured wools, shaded silk embroidery and the first commercially printed linen designs. Common images used were family pets, oriental scenes, flowers and fruit, cherubs, hearts and doves.

BOUQUET BATH TOWEL AND FACE WASHER

MATERIALS

1.05 m (1¼ yd) x 15 cm (6 in) white 14-count Aida cloth
2.4 m (2⅓ yd) x 12 mm (½ in) broderie anglaise eyelet insertion lace
2.15 m (2⅓ yd) x 2.5 cm (1 in) gathered broderie anglaise edging lace
3 m (3¼ yd) x 71 mm (¼ in) matching satin ribbon
1 bath towel and face washer
DMC stranded cottons in the following colours:

225 pale pink
436 coffee cream
552 purple
743 bright yellow
806 teal blue
986 forest green
989 green
3078 pale yellow
3731 deep pink
3733 medium pink

DIRECTIONS

Cut the Aida cloth into two lengths: 75 cm (29½ in) for the towel, and 30 cm (11¾ in) for the face washer. Using the graph in Figure 3.1, work the embroidery in the centre of both strips of Aida cloth and press on the wrong side of the fabric.

The Towel

Lay a strip of insertion lace with ribbon threaded through the eyelet holes vertically across the Aida strip 4 cm (1½ in) from each end and sew in place. Gather and sew the broderie anglaise edging lace across the top and bottom of this Aida strip, turning the outer edges under.

Lay the cross-stitched strip across the towel about 11 cm (4⅓ in) from the bottom edge. Sew this into position, turning the ends under (Figure 3.2).

Thread the ribbon through the eyelet holes of the remaining insertion lace. Place the insertion lace over the join of the Aida strip and the edging lace and machine sew in place, turning the ends under.

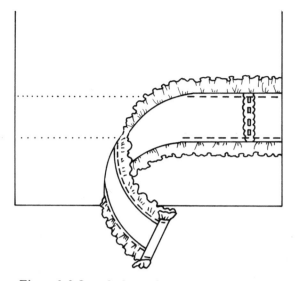

Figure 3.2 Sew the lace-edged Aida strip onto the towel

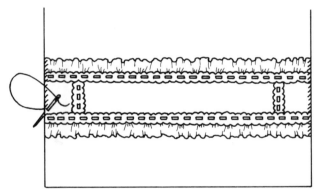

Figure 3.3 Slip stitch the turnings under (towel)

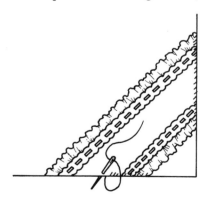

Figure 3.4 Slip stitch the turnings under (washer)

Slip stitch all the turnings under along the edge of the towel (Figure 3.3). Make two small bows and sew them into the centre of the lace borders.

The Face Washer

Lay the strip of Aida cloth diagonally across one corner of the face washer, about 6 cm (2⅓ in) from the edge. Trim the fabric back to 1 cm (⅓ in) from both sides. Fold these turnings under and pin in place before machine sewing the strip across the edges.

Lay the gathered edging lace along both edges of the Aida cloth. Fold in the turnings and machine sew in place. Thread ribbon through the eyelets of the insertion lace and place the lace over the join where the Aida cloth and gathered lace meet. Fold under the turnings and sew in place. Slip stitch all the turnings down to neaten (Figure 3.4).

HEART-SHAPED POTPOURRI SACHET

MATERIALS

21 x 21 cm (8¼ x 8¼ in) black 14-count Aida cloth
21 x 21 cm (8¼ x 8¼ in) black organza
1.5 m (1⅔ yd) x 6 cm (2½ in) black lace
1 m (1¹⁄₁₀ yd) x 7 mm (¼ in) black satin ribbon
1.25 m (1⅓ yd) x 1 cm (⅓ in) black damask ribbon
10 black glass seed beads
DMC stranded cotton in the following colours:

208 deep mauve	892 blush pink
211 pale mauve	894 pale blush pink
321 scarlet	973 yellow
470 light green	996 blue
472 pale green	3052 deep grey-green
523 grey-green	3078 pale yellow
730 dark green	3346 green (includes
742 orange	back stitch stems)
760 deep pink	
761 medium pink	
775 baby blue	

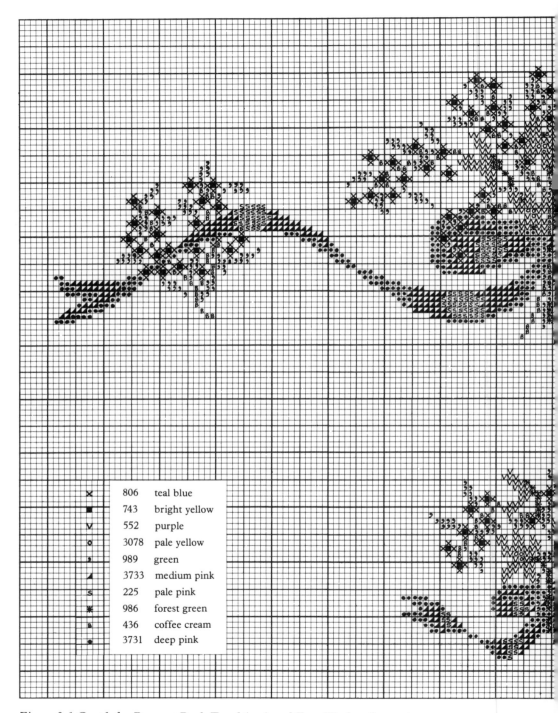

✕	806	teal blue
■	743	bright yellow
⌄	552	purple
◦	3078	pale yellow
,	989	green
◢	3733	medium pink
s	225	pale pink
✱	986	forest green
ʙ	436	coffee cream
●	3731	deep pink

Figure 3.1 Graph for Bouquet Bath Towel (top) and Face Washer (bottom)

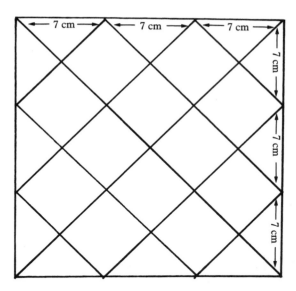

Figure 3.5 Grid for ribbon on Heart-shaped Potpourri Sachet

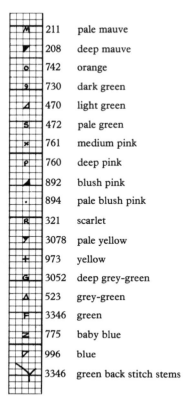

M	211	pale mauve
▼	208	deep mauve
o	742	orange
9	730	dark green
◢	470	light green
S	472	pale green
×	761	medium pink
P	760	deep pink
◢	892	blush pink
·	894	pale blush pink
R	321	scarlet
▼	3078	pale yellow
+	973	yellow
G	3052	deep grey-green
Δ	523	grey-green
F	3346	green
Z	775	baby blue
▽	996	blue
Y	3346	green back stitch stems

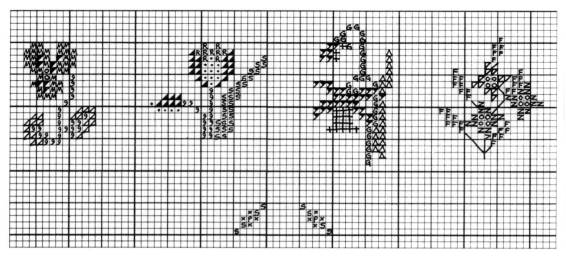

Figure 3.6 Graph for Heart-shaped Potpourri Sachet

62

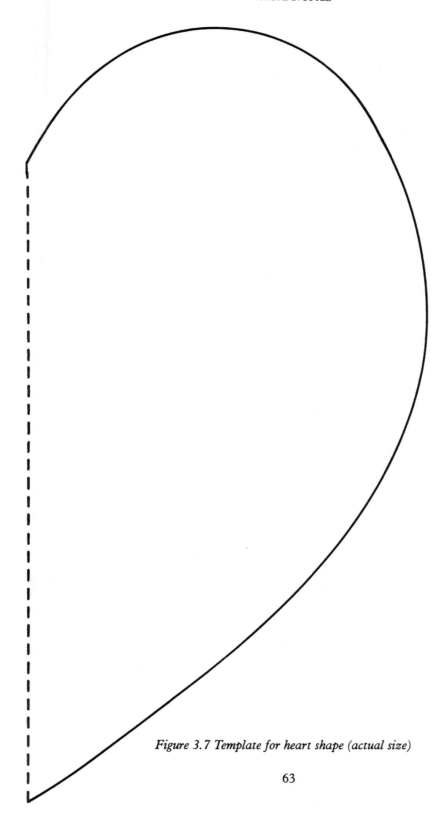

Figure 3.7 Template for heart shape (actual size)

Figure 3.8 Pin template to completed Aida cloth
and cut out

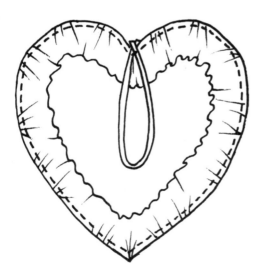

Figure 3.9 Attach lace and loop to heart shape
before adding organza

Figure 3.10 Filled heart shape is slip stitched
closed, then trimmed with bows

DIRECTIONS

Pin the damask ribbon from one corner of the
black Aida cloth to the other. Measure 7 cm
(2¾ in) from the corner and pin the next section
of black ribbon parallel to the first. Measure
the third section of 7 cm (2¾ in) and pin the
ribbon parallel to the first two. Repeat this
process in the other direction until the Aida
square is divided into a grid pattern (Figure
3.5). Catch the ribbon at all the crossing points
with a stitch and a small black bead.

Sew a large floral motif into each of the
central squares and a smaller motif into each

of those squares surrounding them using the graph in Figure 3.6 as a guide.

Once the embroidery is completed, pin the heart-shaped template (Figure 3.7) to the Aida cloth and cut around the edge (Figure 3.8). Zigzag around the raw edge of the fabric to stop it from fraying.

Gather the lace and stitch it around the outside edge of the heart shape. Cut 20 cm (7¾ in) from the plain satin ribbon. Form a loop and sew to the top of the heart (Figure 3.9). Place the organza, also cut in the shape of the heart, face down onto the right side of the cross-stitched fabric. Machine stitch around this edge, leaving an opening for turning.

Turn the heart right side out and fill with potpourri, before slip stitching the opening closed. Cut the remaining length of satin ribbon into 30 cm (11¾ in) for a bow to trim the top of the heart and 50 cm (19¾ in) for a bow at the bottom of the heart. Sew these trims in place (Figure 3.10).

SILK-EMBROIDERED GREETING CARDS

Victorian birthday cards were elaborate affairs with lots of paper lace, bows, coloured and heavily embossed pictures and, of course, sentimental verses. Silk-embroidered cards were usually bought for very special occasions, as although they were machine embroidered, they were also very expensive. Motifs used for this type of card were flowers, butterflies and satin-stitched ribbons and bows.

These modern versions adapted from such earlier cards are embroidered with silk rather than stranded cotton. Silk threads tend to be slippery so are not as easy to work with as the stranded cottons. However, the results are really worth the effort.

As soon as the skein of silk thread has been opened, wind it onto a card securing the end into a small slit. In this way, the thread is controlled and will not have a chance to form a knot. Pull out three strands and wind the remaining three strands onto the card until needed.

MATERIALS

For each card you will need:

32 x 15 cm (12⅔ x 6 in) cream cardboard or 1 commercial blank card

15 x 10 cm (6 x 4 in) cream silk, organza or taffeta

35 cm (13¾ in) cream pearl trim

35 cm (13¾ in) x 12 mm (½ in) cream gathered lace

20 cm (7¾ in) x 3 mm (⅛ in) satin ribbon

Silk embroidery threads

12 x 8 cm (4¾ x 3¼ in) quilt wadding 2 mm (1/16 in) thick

DIRECTIONS

Trace the design onto the fabric using a light marking pen. In an embroidery hoop, stretch the fabric over the quilt wadding. Work the embroidery using three strands of silk through both layers following the designs in Figure 3.11. Sew the motifs using any combination of traditional embroidery stitches, including satin stitch, stem stitch, blanket stitch and lazy daisy stitch.

Press the embroidery very carefully on the wrong side and with a light marking pen or chalk mark the oval aperture (Figure 3.12) on the back of the wadding. Cut away any excess wadding so that only the oval piece at the back of the embroidery remains. When the embroidery is glued onto the card, the oval is slightly padded.

If making your own card, use the measurements in Figure 3.13 as a guide. Cut out the card and score along the lines. Mark the oval aperture onto the centre of the middle panel and carefully cut around this line.

Glue the embroidery onto the centre panel of the card, then fold over the left-hand flap and glue in place (Figure 3.14). Trim any excess fabric from around the edges. Glue the lace around the oval (Figure 3.15). Add the pearls and place the satin ribbon bow at the bottom (Figure 3.16).

Figure 3.11 Designs for Silk-embroidered Greeting Cards

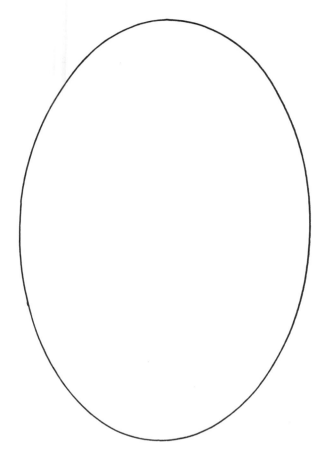

Figure 3.12 Template for oval aperture
(actual size)

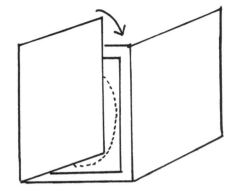

Figure 3.14 Glue the embroidery to centre panel
of card, then fold over and glue left-hand flap

Figure 3.15 Glue lace around the oval

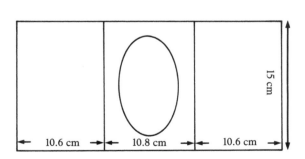

10.6 cm   10.8 cm   10.6 cm

15 cm

Figure 3.13 Measurements for making the card

Figure 3.16 Add pearls and bow

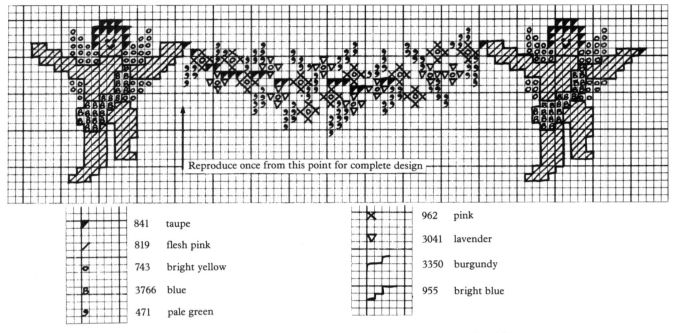

Reproduce once from this point for complete design

	841	taupe
	819	flesh pink
	743	bright yellow
	3766	blue
	471	pale green

	962	pink
	3041	lavender
	3350	burgundy
	955	bright blue

Figure 3.17 Graph for Hearts and Cupids Pillowcases (cupids)

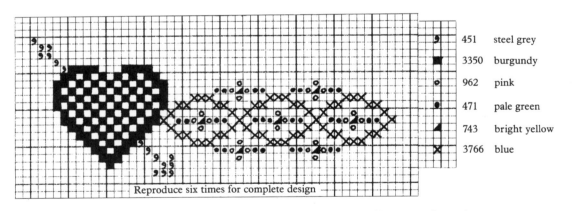

Reproduce six times for complete design

	451	steel grey
	3350	burgundy
	962	pink
	471	pale green
	743	bright yellow
	3766	blue

Figure 3.18 Graph for Hearts and Cupids Pillowcases (hearts)

HEARTS AND CUPIDS PILLOWCASES

MATERIALS

Two white cotton pillowcases

1 m (1 1/10 yd) white 14-count Aida band

1 m (1 1/10 yd) long x 4 cm (1 1/2 in) wide white pre-gathered broderie anglaise lace

1 skein DMC stranded cotton in the following colours:

451 steel grey
471 pale green
743 bright yellow
819 flesh pink
841 taupe
955 bright blue
962 pink
3041 lavender
3350 burgundy
3766 blue

DIRECTIONS

Cut the Aida band in half and following the cross stitch charts provided (Figures 3.17 and 3.18) embroider both pieces, leaving the ends free for turning over later. Iron carefully.

Dissolve a mild detergent in warm water and wash the pillowcases to remove any excess dressing. When dry, iron the pillowcases.

Cut the broderie anglaise lace in half and pin it across the bottom of the pillowcases, turning at least 1 cm (1/3 in) under at each end. Then, keeping the bottom edge of the lace even with the edge of the pillowcase, sew across the top of the lace by machine (Figure 3.19). Hand sew the ends under along the seam lines.

Pin the Aida band over the top edge of the broderie anglaise lace frill, ensuring that at least 1 cm (1/3 in) is turned under at each end. Sew a band across each pillowcase, slip stitching the ends under at the seam lines (Figure 3.20).

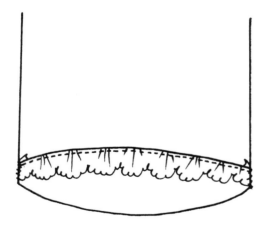

Figure 3.19 Sew lace frill around bottom edge of pillowcase

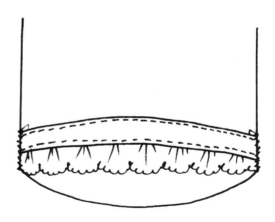

Figure 3.20 Turn under ends of Aida band and slip stitch them to pillowcase seams

German Lutheran Style

Kitchen set (photograph on page 8)
Wedding Sampler and Ring Pillow (photograph on page 9)
Traditional Sampler (photograph on page 10)
Berlin Work Cushion (photograph on page 11)

The German Lutherans who settled in Australia in the mid-nineteenth century created their own farming community in the Barossa Valley in South Australia. Among the skills they introduced were traditional German embroidery styles which were used to decorate practical household items and clothing.

Of the embroidery styles introduced by the German Lutherans in Australia, perhaps the two most important are the sampler and Berlin work.

Samplers are worked on linen in woollen or cotton thread. The German examples from this period feature historical and religious motifs that are embroidered in cross stitch or crewel stitch in muted tones. They reached their peak in popularity in the eighteenth and nineteenth centuries when they were used as a method of teaching young girls to sew. These samplers were hand-hemmed around the edges, often with a different type of hemming on each of the four sides, and contained cross-stitched motifs, the alphabet and numbers. The embroiderer was encouraged to include her name and the completion date on the sampler, adding charm and authenticity to each piece.

During the early nineteenth century, the industrial revolution brought about many changes in embroidery styles. A new technique called Berlin work was developed in Germany and the traditional style of sampler died out. Embroidery designs were printed onto canvas in symbols representing the different colours to be used. The synthetic dyes being formulated meant that a wider range of brightly coloured threads and yarns were available. It is not surprising to find that both the novice and the more experienced embroiderer found these advances inspiring. By the 1850s Berlin work was an established part of household decoration, and patterns for chairs, cushions, rugs, bags, slippers and pictures had been developed to meet the demand. Motifs were inspired by the exotic: animals, birds and flowers from the Orient, Grecian urns and idyllic gardens, and these were generally worked on plain, dark backgrounds.

KITCHEN SET

MATERIALS

1.5 m (1⅔ yd) x 1.15 m (1¼ yd) printed cotton fabric
2 skeins DMC stranded cotton in 311 dark smoky blue
90 cm (1 yd) x 12 cm (4¾ in) white 18-count Aida cloth
2 m (2¼ yd) x 2.5 cm (1 in) white cotton edging lace
50 x 30 cm (19¾ x 11¾ in) quilt wadding
Colour matched sewing machine cotton

DIRECTIONS

Cut the Aida cloth into three lengths: one length of 57 cm (22½ in) and two lengths of 18 cm (7 in). Work the design (Figure 4.1) across the larger piece of Aida cloth leaving an even turning edge of 3 cm (1¼ in) at each end. Choose any section of the border pattern to go across the smaller lengths and work these in cross stitch and back stitch using two strands of cotton across two threads of the Aida cloth. When these have been completed, press them

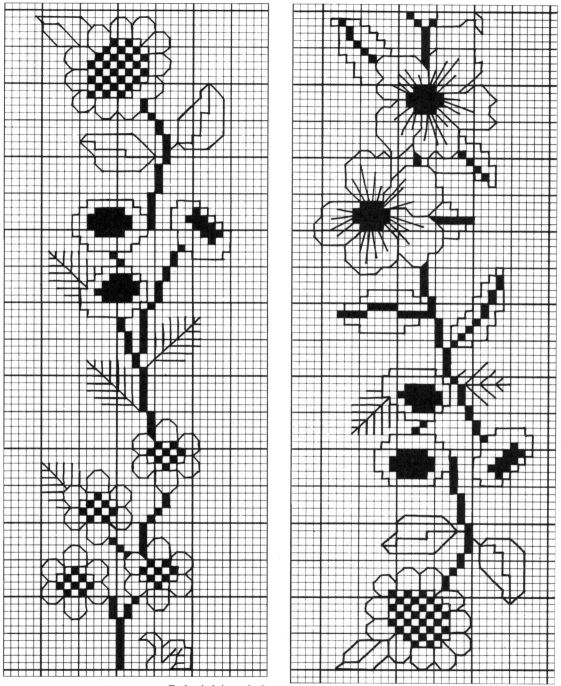

Each stitch is worked over two threads of Aida cloth

Figure 4.1 Graph for Kitchen Set

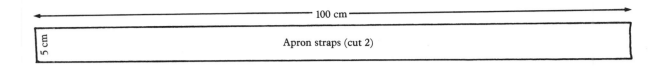

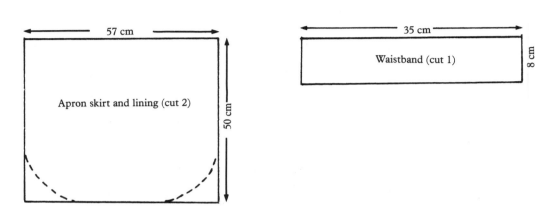

Figure 4.2 Cutting guide for apron

on the wrong side of the embroidery and make up the items as follows.

The Apron

Cut out all the pattern pieces (Figure 4.2). Sew the lace along both edges of the embroidered border with the outer edges together (Figure 4.3). Turn the raw edges inwards and sew the border to the apron using white cotton (Figure 4.4). Place the apron lining right side down onto the right side of the embroidery and stitch around the edge, leaving the top open. Clip the curves if necessary, to give a smooth seam line (Figure 4.5). Turn inside out and press with a moderately hot iron.

Make the apron straps by folding them in half lengthwise and stitching along the edge and across one end. Cut away any excess fabric and turn the straps inside out.

Gather the top of the apron skirt until it will fit the waistband, leaving 1 cm (⅓ in) free

Figure 4.3 Sew lace to embroidered apron border

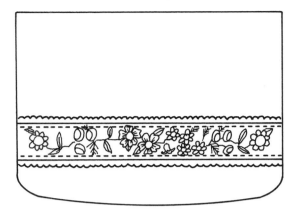

Figure 4.4 Join border to apron

Figure 4.6 Join gathered apron to waistband, leaving 1 cm (½ in) at ends for strap insertion

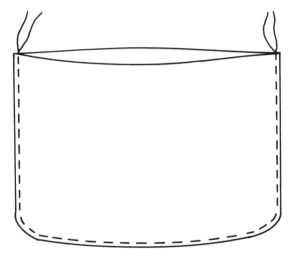

Figure 4.5 Sew lining to apron skirt, leaving top edge open, clipping curves

at each end for the insertion of the straps. With right sides together, sew the gathered skirt to the front waistband edge (Figure 4.6). Fold the band in half and iron the fold line, then fold the waistband over and turn up a 1 cm (⅓ in) seam allowance on the free edge. Slip stitch the back of the waistband to the back of the apron. Turn in the excess fabric at each end of the waistband, insert a strap in each end and, with the strap in place, stitch the opening closed (Figure 4.7).

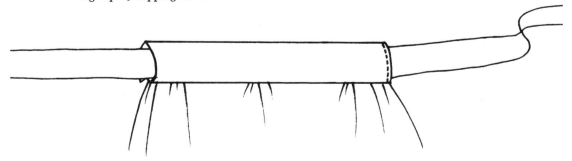

Figure 4.7 Insert and sew straps into waistband

The Pot Holder

Cut out all the pattern pieces and the wadding (Figure 4.8). Stitch the edging lace along the length of the embroidered Aida strip with the outer edges together. Turn the lace outwards and sew the border across the centre of the fabric square (Figure 4.9).

To make the loop, cut a length of material 10 cm (4 in) x 2 cm (¾ in). Fold the sides of the material into the centre, fold in half again and sew close to the edge (Figure 4.10). Attach the loop to the top corner of the front piece of fabric.

Place the wadding onto the wrong side of the backing fabric and machine sew the two together around all four edges (Figure 4.11). Place this padded back right side down onto the right side of the pot holder with the loop between them. The ends of the loop should face outwards at the top corner. Stitch around all four sides leaving an opening on one side for turning right side out (Figure 4.12). Clip away any excess fabric bulk at the corners and turn to the right side before slip stitching the opening closed.

Figure 4.9 Join lace-edged border to fabric square

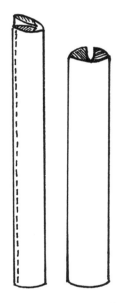

Figure 4.10 Fold and sew pot holder loop

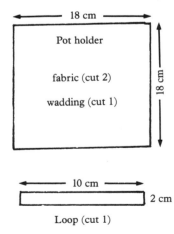

Figure 4.8 Cutting guide for pot holder

Figure 4.11 Join wadding and backing pieces

74

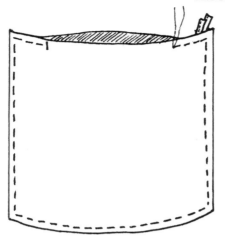

Figure 4.12 Sew back onto front, catching in loops and leaving an opening

The Oven Mitt

From the printed fabric, cut four mitten shapes and from the wadding, cut two mitten shapes (Figure 4.13).

When the Aida strip has been embroidered, sew the strip across the front bottom edge of the mitt. With the top outer edges together, sew the lace to the Aida strip. Turn out the lace so that it is facing upwards and sew the strip down through all layers (Figure 4.14).

With the right sides of the fabric facing out, place the lining, then the wadding and finally the front of the mitt on top of each other. Zigzag around the raw edges to overlock, joining the three layers together. Repeat for the back of the mitt.

With the right sides together, machine sew the front and the back together around the outer edge of the mitt, trim the seam line (Figure 4.15) and clip curves.

Make the loop by folding the sides of the fabric into the centre, then fold over again and sew close to the edge. Pin the loop to the bottom side seam line.

Measure the bottom edge of the mitt and cut a piece of fabric on the cross (Figure 4.16) 3 cm (1¼ in) wide and 1 cm (⅓ in) longer than the measured length. Turn the raw ends under

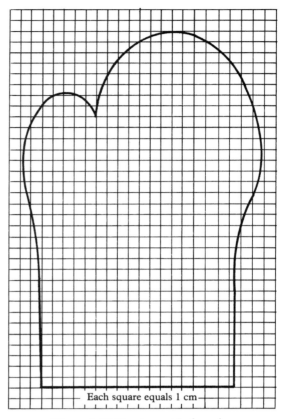

Each square equals 1 cm

Figure 4.13 Cutting guide for mitt

Figure 4.14 Add lace to border strip

75

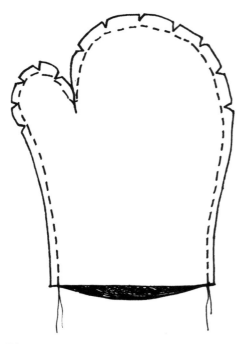

Figure 4.15 Sew front to back of mitt, clipping curves

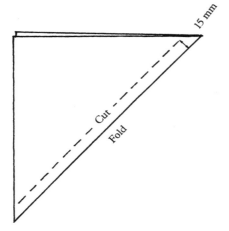

Figure 4.16 Make a bias strip

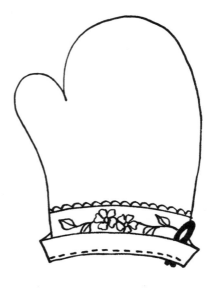

Figure 4.17 Join bias strip and loop to mitt

Figure 4.18 Turn and slip stitch bias binding to bottom of mitt

5 mm (⅕ in) and sew along the seam line. Sew the bias binding around the bottom of the mitt ensuring that right sides are together (Figure 4.17). Turn the binding inwards and slip stitch in place (Figure 4.18).

WEDDING SAMPLER AND RING PILLOW

This sampler records the names of the bride and the groom and the date of the wedding. It incorporates a heart of flowers for love with the doves of peace and the rings of matrimony.

The Wedding Sampler

MATERIALS

45 x 35 cm (17¾ x 13¾ in) white 14-count
Aida cloth
DMC stranded cotton in the following colours:
307 yellow
340 jacaranda
632 brown
742 orange
743 bright yellow
745 pale lemon
826 blue outline of bird on cushion
827 sky blue
937 dark olive green
939 midnight blue outline of bird on sampler
989 green
3713 light pink
3731 deep pink
3733 medium pink
1 reel of DMC Fil or Clair gold metallic
thread

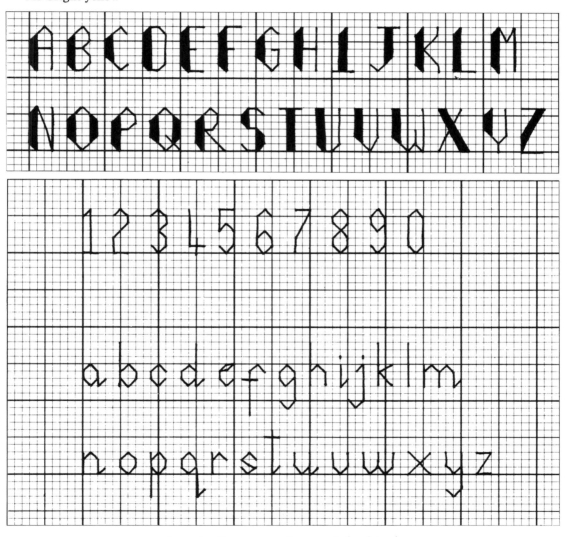

Lettering for names and numerals for dates in
Figure 4.19

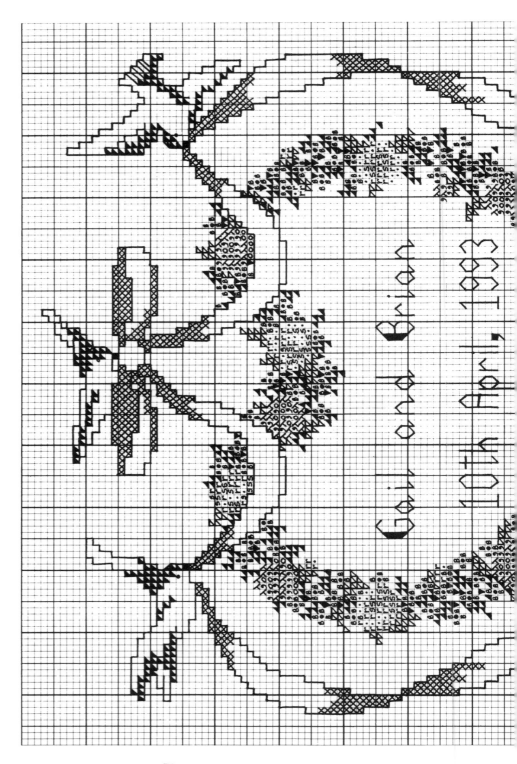

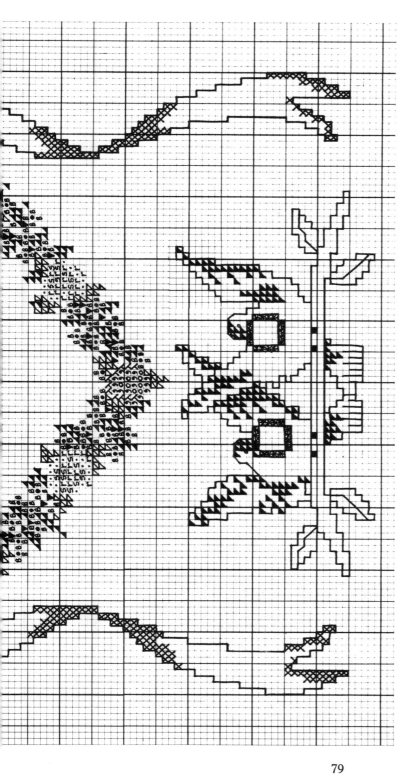

Figure 4.19 Graph for Wedding Sampler

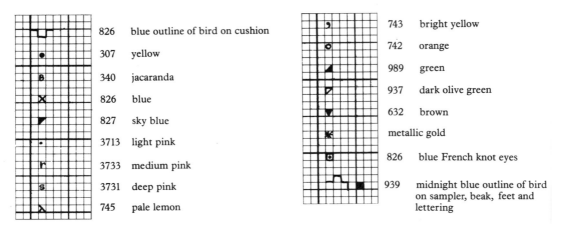

826	blue outline of bird on cushion
307	yellow
340	jacaranda
826	blue
827	sky blue
3713	light pink
3733	medium pink
3731	deep pink
745	pale lemon

743	bright yellow
742	orange
989	green
937	dark olive green
632	brown
	metallic gold
826	blue French knot eyes
939	midnight blue outline of bird on sampler, beak, feet and lettering

Key to Figures 4.19 and 4.20

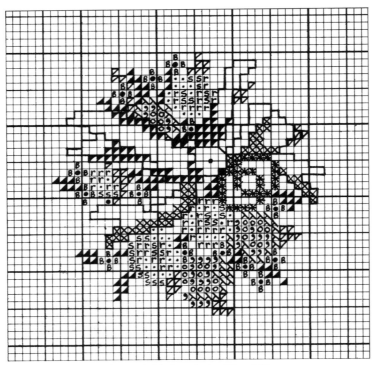

Figure 4.20 Graph for Ring Pillow

DIRECTIONS

To find the centre of the Aida cloth, run a line of horizontal tacking stitches halfway down and a line of vertical tacking stitches halfway across. Where the two lines meet is the centre point.

Following the graph in Figure 4.19, cross stitch from the centre, beginning with the backstitch outline of the ribbon and the birds. When the embroidery is complete, press the sampler very carefully on the wrong side of the work.

The Ring Pillow

MATERIALS

One damask square with an open weave section
in the centre for cross stitch

30 x 30 cm (11¾ x 11¾ in) white satin

1.25m (1⅓ yd) white pre-gathered lace
attached to a straight length of eyelet lace or
1.25 m (1⅓ yd) of each type of lace and sew
the eyelet lace along the gathered edge of
the wider lace

2.5 m (2¾ yd) x 1 cm (⅓ in) white satin
ribbon to fit the eyelet holes in the lace

50 cm (19¾ in) x 1 cm (⅓ in) extra satin
ribbon to tie the rings to the cushion

DIRECTIONS

Cross stitch the bird and flowers in the centre
circle on the damask square following the graph
in Figure 4.20. Press on the wrong side of the
fabric when completed.

Lay the backing satin square face down onto
this damask square and machine sew around
all four sides, leaving an opening on one side,
to turn the pillow inside out.

Turn inside out. Fill the pillow with polyester
wadding and slip stitch the opening closed.
With tiny neat running stitches, sew the line
of the join between the gathered lace and the
straight eyelet lace along the seam line of the
cushion, making small pleats at the four corners
to allow for the right-angle turning. Slip stitch
the top of the eyelet lace to the pillow, then
beginning at the centre front, thread the satin
ribbon through the holes. Tie the ends into a
bow. Stitch the other length of ribbon to the
bird's beak and tie into a bow around the
wedding rings.

TRADITIONAL SAMPLER

MATERIALS

64 x 44 cm (25 x 17 in) cream or white
14-count Aida cloth

1 skein DMC stranded cotton in the following
colours:

223 dusty pink
224 pink
307 bright yellow
310 black
315 cerise
317 charcoal
318 grey
319 forest green
321 vermilion
372 fawn
502 aquamarine
504 pale grey
522 sage green
543 cream
646 steel grey
730 dark green
731 green
734 light green
745 pale lemon
754 baby pink
772 mint green
782 mustard brown
799 cornflower blue
813 sky blue
815 deep red
823 navy blue
839 brown
902 maroon
920 rust
928 soft green
931 blue
932 pale blue
948 flesh pink
972 golden yellow
977 golden orange
3041 lilac
3072 silver grey
3078 pale yellow
3348 lime green
3354 rose pink

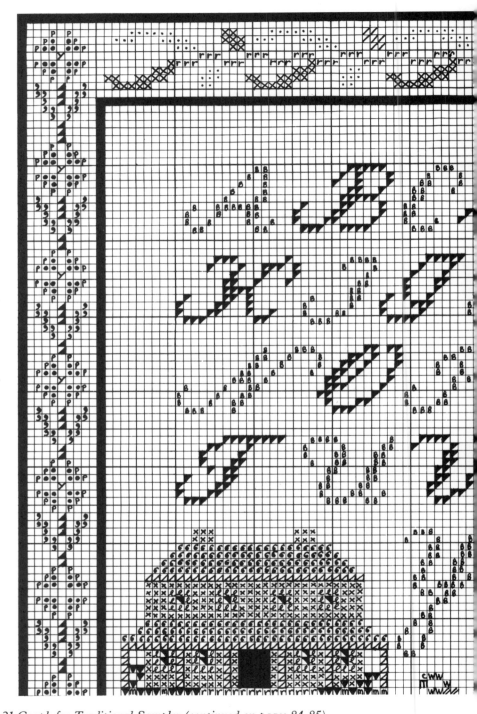

Figure 4.21 Graph for Traditional Sampler (continued on pages 84-85)

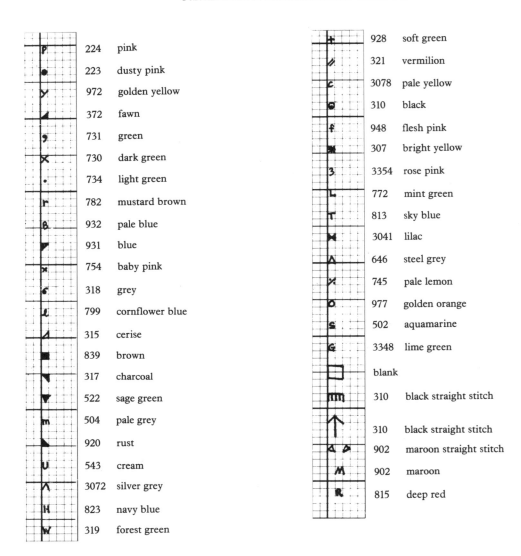

224	pink
223	dusty pink
972	golden yellow
372	fawn
731	green
730	dark green
734	light green
782	mustard brown
932	pale blue
931	blue
754	baby pink
318	grey
799	cornflower blue
315	cerise
839	brown
317	charcoal
522	sage green
504	pale grey
920	rust
543	cream
3072	silver grey
823	navy blue
319	forest green

928	soft green
321	vermilion
3078	pale yellow
310	black
948	flesh pink
307	bright yellow
3354	rose pink
772	mint green
813	sky blue
3041	lilac
646	steel grey
745	pale lemon
977	golden orange
502	aquamarine
3348	lime green
	blank
310	black straight stitch
310	black straight stitch
902	maroon straight stitch
902	maroon
815	deep red

Key to Figure 4.21

DIRECTIONS

Begin by marking the centre of the Aida cloth. To do this, run a line of tacking stitches halfway down and a line of vertical stitches halfway across the fabric. Where the two lines meet is the centre point.

Following the graph in Figure 4.21, work the border first, then fill in the motifs, beginning with the alphabet at the top.

When the embroidery is completed, remove the tacking stitches and press on the wrong side.

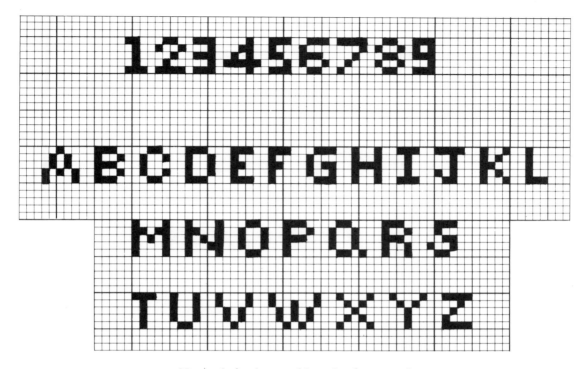

Numerals for dates and lettering for names in
Figure 4.21

BERLIN WORK CUSHION

MATERIALS

50 x 50 cm (19¾ x 19¾ in) Penelope or double
  weave tapestry canvas
40 x 40 cm (15¾ x 15¾ in) heavy backing
  fabric such as wool or velvet
Cushion wadding
DMC tapestry wool in the following colours:
10 skeins of background colour:
7297 dark smoky blue
1 skein each of:
7110 maroon
7195 salmon pink
7198 burgundy
7210 lilac
7251 pale mauve
7255 lavender
7257 purple
7364 olive green

7393 dark green
7401 rust
7436 golden orange
7437 orange
7439 burnt orange
7468 chocolate brown
7496 fawn
7504 mustard
7510 ivory
7514 brown
7544 deep red
7583 lime green
7606 scarlet
7666 red
7677 khaki
7725 custard yellow
7745 cream
7783 honey
7988 emerald green

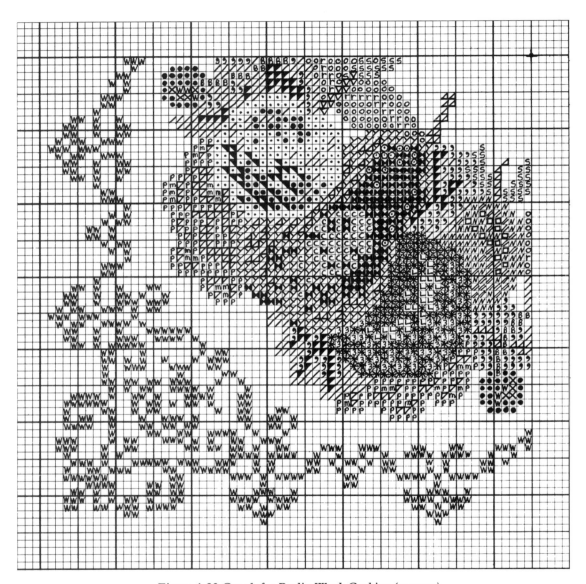

Figure 4.23 Graph for Berlin Work Cushion (quarter)

5	7364	olive green
/	7583	lime green
B	7468	chocolate brown
o	7988	emerald green
r	7401	rust
S	7677	khaki
●	7544	deep red
◤	7393	dark green
▽	7514	brown
X	7666	red
W	7510	ivory
·	7606	scarlet
◢	7496	fawn
Y	7504	mustard

p	7257	purple
m	7251	pale mauve
◤	7255	lavender
◥	7198	burgundy
◢	7725	custard yellow
⊙	7783	honey
c	7745	cream
✳	7437	orange
L	7436	golden orange
3	7439	burnt orange
N	7110	maroon
/	7210	lilac
◘	7195	salmon pink

Key to Figure 4.23

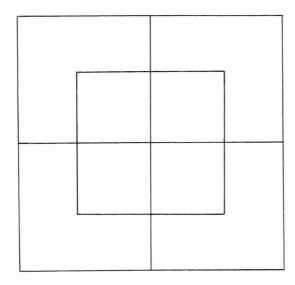

Figure 4.22 Placement of the four quarters of the Berlin Work Cushion

DIRECTIONS

With a blue pencil or a felt-tipped pen that is a similar shade to the background colour, find the centre of the canvas by running vertical and horizontal lines halfway across and halfway down. Also mark the four corner squares so that the pattern can be correctly positioned (Figure 4.22).

Enlarge the quarter pattern graph (Figure 4.23) on a photocopier so that it is easier to read.

Work a quarter of the design at a time, turning the pattern around for each direction. Do not change the direction of the stitching though, as the stitches must always lie in the same manner.

When the canvas has been completed, stretch the dampened work onto a frame until it has dried smooth and firm.

Trim away the excess canvas from around the sides, leaving a 1.5 cm (½ in) turning and lay the backing fabric on the embroidery, ensuring that right sides are together. Machine stitch around three sides of the square. Clip away the fabric at the corners and turn the cushion inside out. Pull gently on the corners to make them square. Fill the cushion with the wadding until it is plump, then slip stitch the open side closed with matching blue thread.

Federation Style

Federation House Cross Stitch (photograph on page 12)
Patchwork Doily (photograph on page 12)
Apple Blossom Pictures (photograph on page 13)
Quilted Wildflower Placemats (photograph on page 12)

The strong patriotic emotions that were prevalent at the time of Australia's federation in 1901 infiltrated many different areas of the Australian way of life. Embroidery did not escape attention and printed linen designs proudly displayed maps of Australia, wildflowers and animals, and slogans such as 'Advance, Australia Fair', 'Greetings from Australia' and 'Australia, Our Home'. One popular design from this era was a handkerchief sachet in the shape of Australia decorated with gum blossoms. The earlier examples of embroidery designs which concentrated on the flowers of English gardens were giving way to local wildflowers such as wattle, gum blossoms and bottlebrush. Embroiderers were identifying with the new designs, using stitches which more closely resembled the form of the flower, such as long straight stitches with a small French knot at the end for gum blossom and blanket stitch circles for wattle.

FEDERATION HOUSE CROSS STITCH

MATERIALS

55 x 40 cm (21⅓ x 16¾ in) white 14-count Aida cloth
1 skein DMC stranded cotton in the following colours:
221 maroon
223 dusty pink
224 pink
300 brown
310 black (outline of roof and veranda)
326 crimson
327 purple
436 coffee cream
504 mint green
524 pale green
612 fawn
640 light brown
676 mustard
677 pale buff
730 dark green
732 olive green
733 lime green
746 cream
928 ice blue
930 deep smoky blue
932 light smoky blue
938 chocolate
3041 lavender
3042 lilac

DIRECTIONS

Tape the edges or zigzag around all four sides of the Aida cloth to prevent fraying. Run a row of vertical and horizontal tacking stitches halfway across and halfway down to find the centre point. Begin working the design from this position following the graph in Figure 5.1. When the cross stitch is completed, press on the wrong side of the work and prepare for framing.

PATCHWORK DOILY

Patterns and designs for doilies proliferated in this country from the 1890s until the 1950s. The more popular designs were produced by Madame Weigel in Melbourne and her patterns

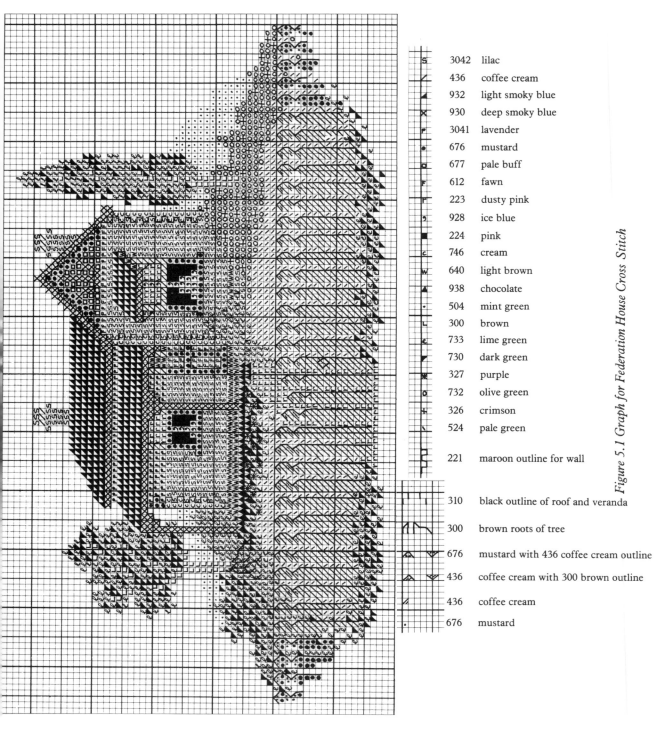

	3042	lilac
	436	coffee cream
	932	light smoky blue
	930	deep smoky blue
	3041	lavender
	676	mustard
	677	pale buff
	612	fawn
	223	dusty pink
	928	ice blue
	224	pink
	746	cream
	640	light brown
	938	chocolate
	504	mint green
	300	brown
	733	lime green
	730	dark green
	327	purple
	732	olive green
	326	crimson
	524	pale green
	221	maroon outline for wall
	310	black outline of roof and veranda
	300	brown roots of tree
	676	mustard with 436 coffee cream outline
	436	coffee cream with 300 brown outline
	436	coffee cream
	676	mustard

Figure 5.1 Graph for Federation House Cross Stitch

appeared in several women's magazines and journals as well as on sheets and booklets available from haberdashery stores.

Collections of original pre-war doilies are now eagerly sought and there is a method of salvaging sections of worn and stained doilies which involves sewing them together in a form of crazy patchwork. In this way, only the ruined pieces of embroidered linen need be disposed of and the colourful good areas are retained for a delightful record of days gone by.

For those who don't have access to original doilies but who would like to create the effect of a patchwork doily cushion, picture, quilt or traycloth, it is simply a matter of cheating. Use a single piece of linen divided into several areas and trace a small traditional design into each. These areas can be edged with lace or strips of original crocheted edging from a discarded, perhaps badly stained, doily.

MATERIALS

50 x 40 cm (19¾ x 16¾ in) cream linen
50 x 40 cm (19¾ x 16¾ in) cream backing fabric
2 m (2¼ yd) cream lace edging
Odd lengths of lace, coloured edgings and braids
Scraps of many different shades of stranded cotton
Suitable small motifs to be traced or ironed on.

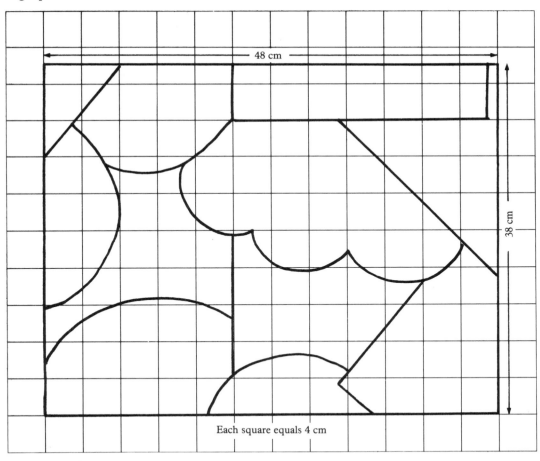

Figure 5.2 Pattern for crazy patches

Figure 5.3 Motifs for doily patches

DIRECTIONS

Enlarge the patterns for the crazy patches and trace these lines onto the linen (Figure 5.2). Place a suitably sized motif (Figure 5.3) to be embroidered into each area, either by tracing or by ironing on a commercial transfer.

The cross stitch motifs can be embroidered over waste canvas which is removed once the work has been completed. Cut a piece of waste canvas slightly larger than the motif to be cross stitched and tack it to the background fabric. Cross stitch through the evenly woven holes of the waste canvas and when the motif is completed, dampen the work slightly to dissolve the glue. Remove the tacking stitches.

Use several different colours of cottons to make the patches appear authentic and finish off each area by handstitching onto it a piece of lace edging or by blanket stitching or satin stitching an embroidered edge along the marked line.

Slip stitch the ends of the lace edgings down flat, and press the traycloth on the wrong side. Pin the lace edging around the outer edges allowing a little fullness at the corners. Sew the two ends of the lace neatly together by hand. With right sides together, lay the backing fabric on the traycloth. Ensure that the lace is tacked towards the centre of the traycloth so that it will not get caught in the stitching. Sew around all four sides, leaving an opening for turning it inside out. Clip away any excess fabric at the corners and turn out the traycloth to the right side. Neatly slip stitch the opening closed.

APPLE BLOSSOM PICTURES

MATERIALS

2 pieces of pale green furnishing fabric or satin or taffeta. Cut one piece 20 x 20 cm (7¾ x 7¾ in) and the other 18 x 18 cm (7 x 7 in)
1 skein each DMC stranded cotton in the following colours:
726 yellow
745 pale lemon
760 deep pink
761 pink
840 light brown
844 charcoal
3024 silver-grey
3346 green
3347 medium green
3348 light green
3770 pale pink

DIRECTIONS

Transfer or trace the appropriate design (Figures 5.4 and 5.5) onto the centre of each fabric square. Working in three strands of cotton throughout, embroider the flower petals in long and short stitch. Start with deep pink nearest the flower centre, then use pink and finally pale pink around the edges. The centre of the flowers is a circle of light green blanket stitch with a scattering of yellow French knots over the top. Work the stems and leaf veins in stem stitch and the leaves in the three shades of green. The butterfly wings in the larger picture are in long and short stitch. The inner edge of the wings are worked in pale lemon, the middle is silver-grey and the outer edge is charcoal. The body is embroidered in charcoal

Figure 5.4 Design for Apple Blossom Picture (1)

Figure 5.5 Design for Apple Blossom Picture (2)

satin stitch and the antennae in charcoal stem stitch. The legs are small charcoal straight stitches.

Cut two pieces of backing cardboard, the larger one measuring 10.5 x 10 cm (4¼ x 4 in) and the smaller one measuring 9 x 8.5 cm (3½ x 3⅓ in) and lace the fabric over these before framing.

QUILTED WILDFLOWER PLACEMATS

These Wildflower placemats have been embroidered with designs representing four of the most well-known Australian wildflowers.

MATERIALS

40 cm (15¾ in) x 120 cm (1⅓ yd) cream quilted calico, available from most patchwork fabric suppliers

6 m (6½ yd) cream cotton lace edging 3 cm (1¼ in) wide

1 skein each DMC stranded cotton in the following colours:

Bottlebrush (Figure 5.6)
Pollen
310 black (use 1 strand)
Flowers
321 scarlet (use 2 strands), 815 maroon (use 2 strands)
Leaves
469 green (use 3 strands)
Stem
841 taupe (use 3 strands)
Stem within flowers
3348 light green (use 3 strands)

Blue Leschenaultia (Figure 5.7)
Stem
301 rust (use 3 strands)
Flowers
806 teal blue (use 3 strands)
Centres
907 light green (use 3 strands)
Leaves
3345 dark green (use 3 strands)

Wattle (Figure 5.8)
Stem
301 rust (use 3 strands)
Leaves
469 green (use 3 strands)
Flowers
743 bright yellow (use 3 strands), 902 dark
  yellow (use 3 strands)

Gum Blossoms (Figure 5.9)
Leaves
469 green (use 3 strands), 523 grey-green (use
  3 strands)
Pollen
743 bright yellow (use 2 strands)
Stem for leaves
841 taupe (use 3 strands)
Stem for flowers
3348 light green (use 3 strands)
Flowers
3706 lolly pink (use 2 strands)

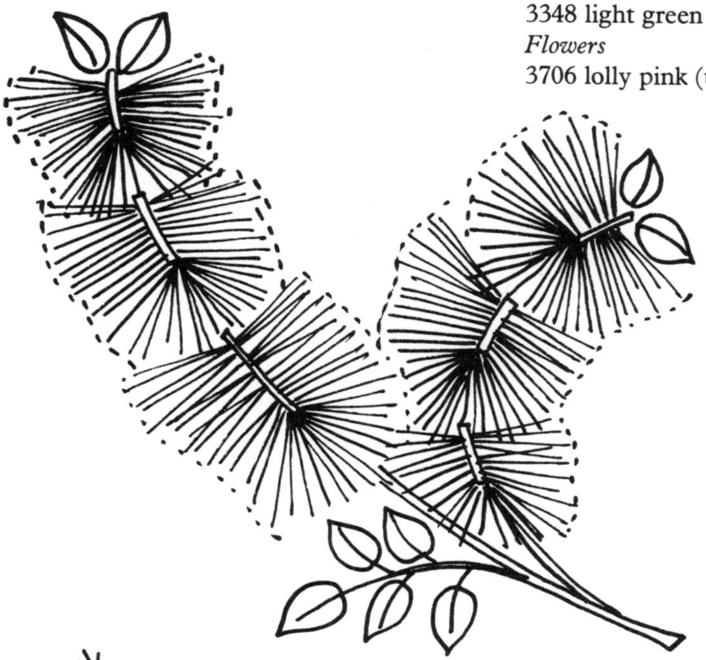

Figure 5.6 Design for Bottlebrush Quilted Placemat

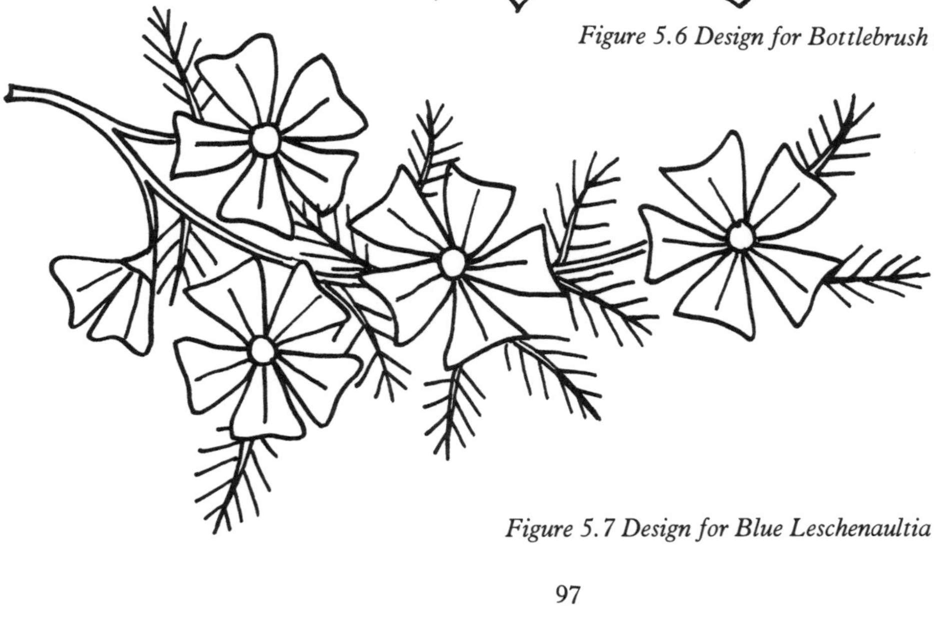

Figure 5.7 Design for Blue Leschenaultia Quilted Placemat

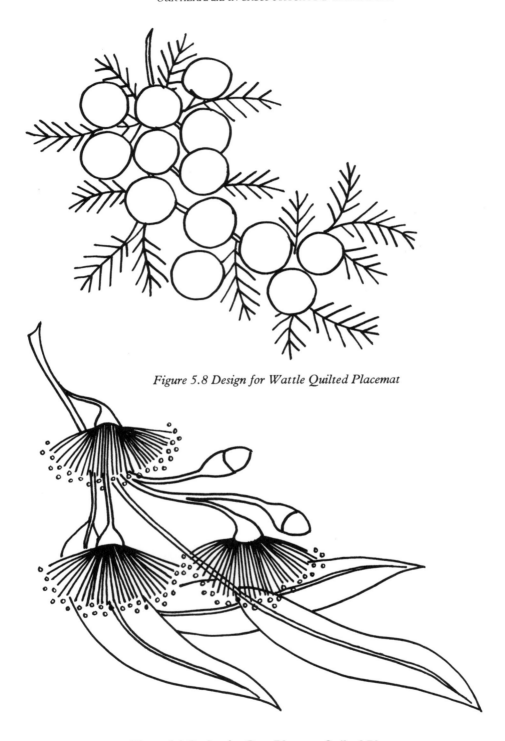

Figure 5.8 Design for Wattle Quilted Placemat

Figure 5.9 Design for Gum Blossoms Quilted Placemat

DIRECTIONS

Cut out the four placemats following Figure 5.10. Using Figures 5.11 and 5.12 as a guide, round off the corners. Zigzag closely around the edges. Cut the lace edging into four even lengths, gather and machine stitch one length around each placemat, allowing more fullness at the corners (Figure 5.13). Neatly slip stitch the ends of the lace together so that it won't fray while the embroidery is being worked.

Using dressmaker's carbon paper, transfer a floral design (Figures 5.6, 5.7, 5.8, 5.9) onto one corner of each placemat and embroider in the following manner: the leaves in satin stitch and straight stitch, the stems in stem stitch, the gum blossoms in straight stitch, the pollen in French knots, the wattle and leschenaultia flowers in blanket stitch, the bottlebrush flowers in stem stitch, the leschenaultia centres in straight stitch.

Press the placemats on the wrong side with a cool iron (calico does tend to scorch easily if ironed with a hot iron).

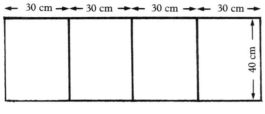

Figure 5.10 Cutting guide for placemats

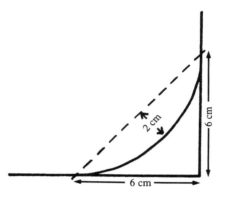

Figure 5.12 Guide for rounding off corner (close-up)

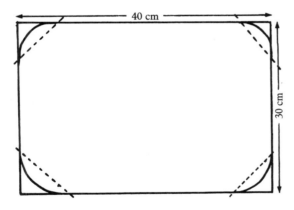

Figure 5.11 Guide for rounding off corners

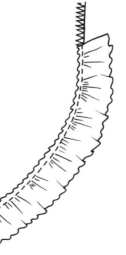

Figure 5.13 Join lace frill to zigzagged mat edges

99

European Influence

Whitework Cushion (photograph on page 14)
Blackwork Banksia Picture (photograph on page 15)
Cutwork Runner (photograph on page 16)
Trapunto Quilted Jewellery Roll (photograph on page 14)

European embroidery has its roots in the church and Italy in particular has been one of the leading producers of fine silk threads and fabrics since the middle ages. Ecclesiastical embroidery relied heavily on the embellishing techniques using metallic gold and silver threads and many European religious communities still use rich colours and gilded artforms.

In the twentieth century the increasing number of European immigrants in Australia has led to new embroidery styles being introduced. Whitework, Blackwork and Cutwork have been readily adapted by Australian embroiderers and used on pictures, cushions, runners, bed linen and clothes.

WHITEWORK CUSHION

MATERIALS

42 x 42 cm (16½ x 16½ in) white even-weave linen, 8 threads per cm (18 threads per in)
6 skeins DMC Broder special thread in white
2 skeins DMC Coton perle in white
3.5 m (3¾ yd) x 6 cm (2⅓ in) white cotton lace
84 x 42 cm (33 x 16½ in) cream backing fabric such as homespun or calico
Polyester filling for the finished cushion

DIRECTIONS

Zigzag stitch or tape the four raw edges of the linen to avoid fraying. Run a row of vertical and horizontal tacking stitches halfway across and halfway down to find the centre.

· Measure 9 cm in from the outer edge on all four sides, then embroider satin stitch over four threads around the four sides (Figure 6.1). Start with a mitred corner and work over 212 threads and finish with another mitred corner (Figure 6.2). Turn the corner and repeat down the second side. When all four sides have been satin stitched, embroider the grid pattern across the centre, allowing fifty threads for each square. Fill each square with the corresponding stitch given.

1 Eight-sided stitch (Figure 6.3).
2 Double ladder hem stitch border around buttonholed square (see Stitches, page 115).
3 Alternate satin stitch over two threads (Figure 6.4).
4 Cutwork flower motif (Figure 6.5).
5 Interlaced hem stitch, twisted through the centre (see Stitches, page 116).
6 Cushion stitch (Figure 6.6).
7 Pinwheel centre on sixteen spokes (Figure 6.7).
8 Four-sided stitch over four threads (see Stitches, page 115).
9 Chequered satin stitch over five threads (Figure 6.8).
10 Butterfly motif, filling stitched wings (Figure 6.9).
11 Florentine satin stitch (Figure 6.10).
12 Woven bars — draw out alternate four threads (Figure 6.11).
13 Pulled eyelet holes around buttonholed centre (Figure 6.12).
14 Reversed four-sided stitch (see Stitches, page 115).
15 Woven bars — nine stitches over four threads (Figure 6.13).
16 Chequered satin stitch over four threads (see Stitches, page 116).

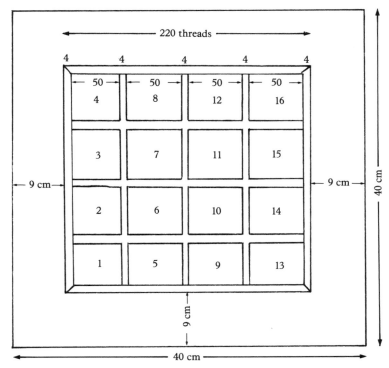

Figure 6.1 Placement guide for satin stitching over four threads

Figure 6.2 Outer border pattern of cushion grid with mitred corner

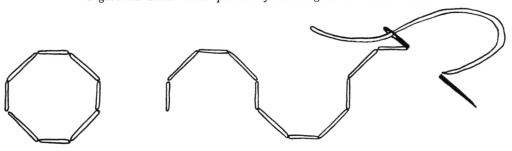

Figure 6.3 Eight-sided stitch

Figure 6.4 Alternate satin stitch over two threads

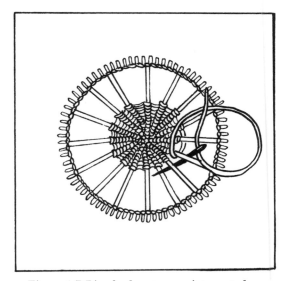

Figure 6.7 Pinwheel centre on sixteen spokes

Figure 6.5 Cutwork flower motif

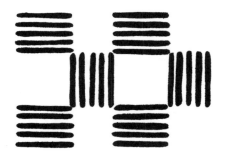

Figure 6.8 Chequered satin stitch over five threads

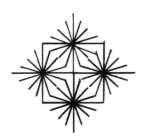

Figure 6.6 Cushion stitch (diamond eyelet stitch)

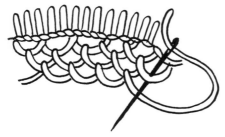

Figure 6.9 Butterfly motif and filling stitch for wings

Figure 6.10 Florentine satin stitch

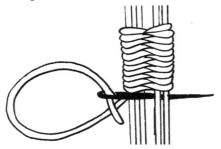

Figure 6.11 Woven bars, drawing out alternate four threads

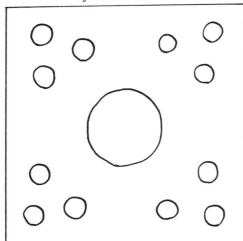

Figure 6.12 Centre circle and eyelets; oversewing an eyelet

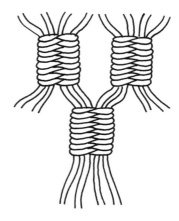

Figure 6.13 Woven bars, nine stitches over four threads

When this is completed, pull the tacking stitches from the fabric and iron carefully on the wrong side.

Cut the backing fabric into two separate squares measuring 42 x 42 cm (16½ x 16½ in) and baste one square behind the whitework embroidery.

Gather the lace to form a frill that will fit around the four edges. Sew the two ends together neatly by hand. Pin, tack and sew the lace frill to the cushion front.

To prevent the lace frill from being caught in the seam as the back is sewn onto the front, sew a rough gathering thread around the scalloped edge of the lace and pull in towards the centre of the cushion. Lay the backing piece face down onto the right side of the cushion front and sew around the top and both sides. Trim any excess fabric away from the corners and turn inside out. Remove the gathering thread. Fill the cushion with the polyester wadding and slip stitch the bottom edge closed.

BLACKWORK BANKSIA PICTURE

Blackwork is counted thread embroidery worked in black yarn onto an evenly woven linen fabric. Often referred to as Spanish Blackwork, this type of embroidery was popular among aristocratic members of sixteenth century Europe, who used it to decorate clothing, such as collars and frilled cuffs, caps, shirt sleeves and aprons. The black stitching may have been highlighted with gold and silver thread to show wealth and status.

Gradually as fabrics such as coarsely woven linens became more readily available, the fashion for blackwork changed to household items such as chair backs, cushions, lampshades, curtain borders and pictures.

Blackwork was introduced in Australia by the Italian immigrant women of the late-nineteenth century who used it to decorate household items and clothes.

MATERIALS
55 x 45 cm (21²/₃ x 17¾ in) white even-weave linen, 8 threads per cm (18 threads per in)
4 skeins DMC stranded cotton in black
1 reel of DMC Fil or Clair gold metallic thread

DIRECTIONS
Run a vertical and a horizontal tacking thread halfway across and halfway down the fabric to find the centre point. Commence the embroidery from this point. The solid lines in Figure 6.14 are to be worked in three strands of black thread and for the dotted lines use three strands of gold thread.

CUTWORK RUNNER

Cutwork, sometimes referred to as *Richelieu* work, was a popular embroidery style in sixteenth- and seventeenth-century Italy and Spain.

During the late-nineteenth and early-twentieth centuries, affluent women who had access to fine linens and plenty of time to embroider became adept at creating beautiful tablecloths, doilies, runners, chair backs, tea-cosies and pillowcases.

Generally cutwork is associated with whitework, in which both the background fabric and the threads used for embroidery are white. In some areas of Italy, however, a single colour sewn onto a white background is popular. The most commonly used colours are red, blue and black.

MATERIALS
35 x 90 cm (13¾ x 35½ in) white finely woven linen
6 skeins DMC stranded cotton in 775 pale blue

DIRECTIONS
Trace the design (Figure 6.15) onto the fabric reversing the pattern to form the design at the other end. Mark the fabric crosswise and lengthwise (Figure 6.16). Using white thread, sew small running stitches along all lines of the pattern, then with two strands of blue cotton work fine buttonhole stitches over these. Make sure that all sections to be cut out have the backs of the buttonhole stitches facing them.

When the buttonhole stitches are completed, including the buttonhole bars between the flowers and the straight edges, carefully cut out the spaces at either end of the runner, keeping close to the buttonhole stitches.

Press the runner on the wrong side of the work. When not in use, roll it around a cardboard cylinder to avoid unnecessary creasing.

Work in three strands of black stranded cotton

Work in gold thread

Figure 6.14 Graph for Blackwork Banksia Picture

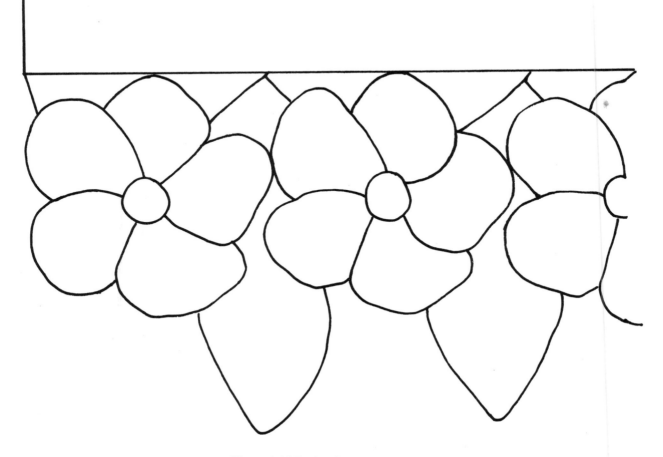

Figure 6.15 Design for Cutwork Runner

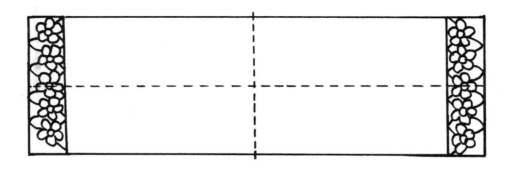

Figure 6.16 Mark the fabric lengthwise and crosswise

TRAPUNTO QUILTED JEWELLERY ROLL

This small and compact jewellery pouch has several pockets to hold chains and pendants and will accommodate four rows of earrings on the ribbon bands. It can be tucked into a corner of a dressing-table drawer and is an invaluable aid to travellers, fitting snugly into a pocket of a suitcase, keeping rings and other small items of jewellery safe and secure.

Trapunto or corded quilting is made from two parallel lines that are stitched around a design. The area between the stitches is raised by threading cord through from the back of the work.

Quilting is often used in conjunction with trapunto work. Small stitches are worked around the design in a single line, the back of each section is slit and a small piece of wadding is inserted to create the padded effect. When this is completed the slit at the back is sewn closed.

MATERIALS

4 pieces of satin 38 x 22 cm (15 x 8⅔ in)
2 pieces of satin 7.5 x 18 cm (3 x 7 in)
1 piece of quilt wadding 38 x 22 cm
   (15 x 8⅔ in)
2 m (2¼ yd) thin cord or thick cotton yarn
Small amount of quilt wadding to pad the fan
   shape
Silk or ribbon roses and narrow ribbon bow for
   trimming
25 cm (10 in) x 3 mm (⅒ in) narrow satin
   ribbon for the tie
88 x 2 cm (34⅔ x ¾ in) satin ribbon, cut into
   four equal lengths.

DIRECTIONS

Trace the design (Figure 6.17) for the jewellery pouch onto one piece of satin 38 x 22 cm (15 x 8⅔ in) on the wrong side of the material. Tack this piece of satin to another piece the same size, matching the corners. Work a single row of tiny running stitches around each section of the fan shape. When this has been completed, work a double row of lines along the grid lines.

From the back of the material thread cording or yarn through the parallel lines of the diagonal grid (Figure 6.18). Pad each section of the fan separately, slip stitching the openings closed as each area is worked (Figure 6.19).

To make the inner lining, lay the other two pieces of satin 38 x 22 cm (15 x 8⅔ in) together with the quilt wadding between them and tack around the edges. Make two hemmed pockets approximately 5 cm (2 in) deep and stitch them across the bottom of the inner pouch, one above the other. Evenly space the four pieces of satin ribbon across the upper half of the inner pouch and sew them at each end. Sew down the centre through the ribbon and the pockets. Then sew through the pockets on each side of the centre line, dividing each layer into four separate pockets (Figure 6.20).

Sew around the edges of the quilted fan design. Pin one length of the narrow ribbon to the end of this section of the pouch, facing inwards (Figure 6.21).

With right sides facing, place the two pieces of the pouch together and sew around three sides. Trim away any excess fabric from the sides and the corners.

Turn inside out and slip stitch the open side closed. Stitch the other piece of narrow ribbon to the centre of the plain end of the pouch, measuring 9 cm (3½ in) from the bottom edge.

Trim with silk or ribbon roses, satin ribbon bows and optional seed pearls dotted over the fan.

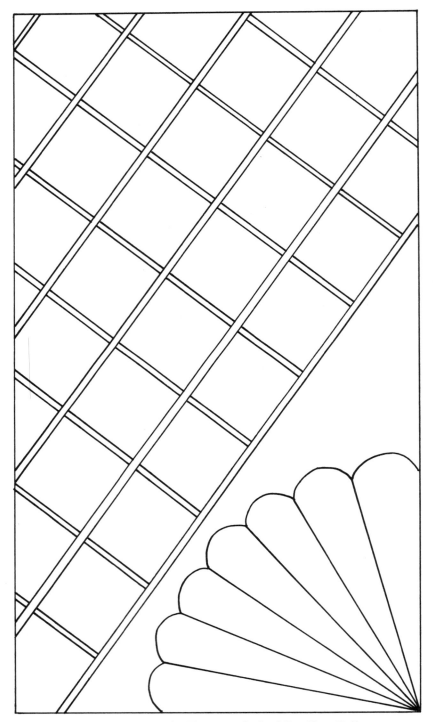

Figure 6.17 Design for Trapunto Quilted Jewellery Roll

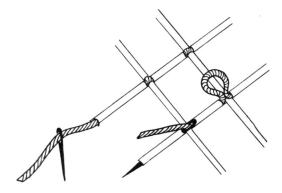

Figure 6.18 Thread cord through the parallel lines of the grid

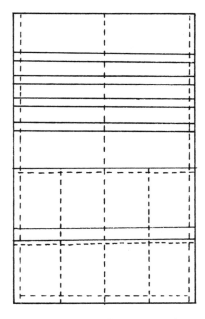

Figure 6.20 Inner view of pouch showing positions of pockets and ribbons

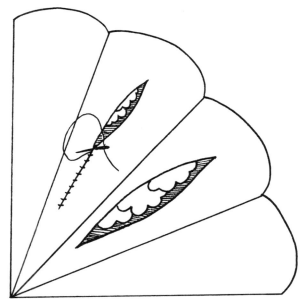

Figure 6.19 Pad each section of fan and slip stitch it closed

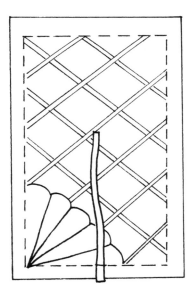

Figure 6.21 Sew round edges of fan with ribbon tie pinned in place

Stitches

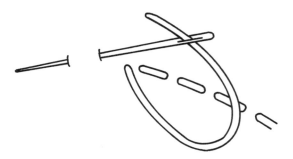

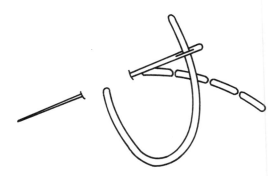

RUNNING STITCH

Small stitches of even length, useful for outlining and filling areas which are to be padded.

BACK STITCH

A flat straight stitch used mainly for outlines, especially when combined with counted thread work such as cross stitch.

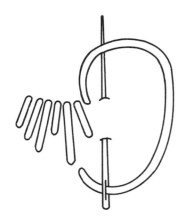

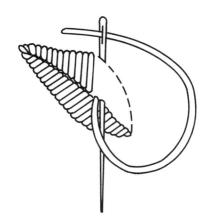

SATIN STITCH

Straight stitches lying close together to cover an area completely. They should be worked on a taut fabric so that the tension remains even, as this stitch tends to pull if done too tightly.

STRAIGHT STITCH

Single flat stitches of regular or irregular lengths, useful for stamens of flowers, grass, fur of animals and feathers.

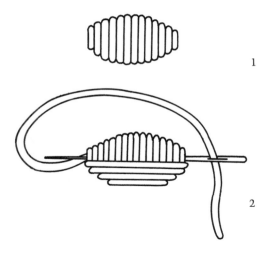

1

2

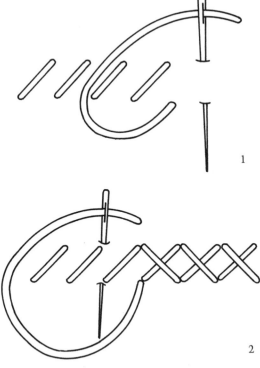

1

2

PADDED SATIN STITCH

Where a raised surface is required, work two layers of satin stitches in opposite directions, the first layer being the padding.

CROSS STITCH

Working from left to right, sew the first half of the cross stitch to the end of the row, then reverse the direction to complete the crosses. Sew single stitches in the same way. Ensure that on the back of the work the cross stitch is straight, not angled.

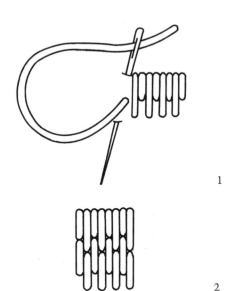

1

2

LONG AND SHORT STITCH

Long and short alternated satin stitches are worked in the first row only, followed by rows of even length stitches. This is suitable for filling in large areas of shaded stitchery.

STEM STITCH

Again worked from left to right, this stitch is used for outlines, however, several rows worked close together make an attractive filling stitch. Keep the thread always to the left of the needle and the stitches of an even length.

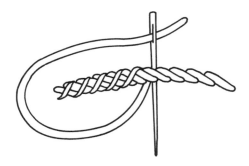

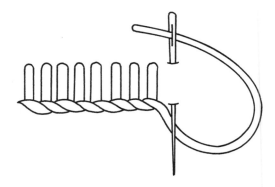

WHIPPED STEM STITCH

After completing an initial row of stem stitch, take the thread *over* and the needle *under* each stitch making sure that you do not catch the fabric underneath. The whipping thread can be a different colour if desired.

BLANKET OR BUTTONHOLE STITCH

Blanket stitch differs from buttonhole stitch as the stitches are worked a little way apart from one another. Sewn close together, this forms the basis of cutwork embroidery. Work from top to bottom keeping the thread under the needle.

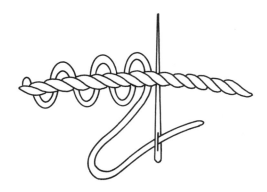

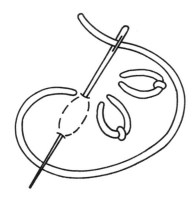

THREADED STEM STITCH

Complete a row of stem stitch, then with another thread take the needle under the stem stitch from one side to the other, leaving a small even loop.

LAZY DAISY STITCH

Single basic chain stitches, sometimes worked over a straight stitch first, form petals of a daisy, small leaves, rain drops and centres of larger flowers. Once the chain is formed, place the needle through the fabric on the outside of the chain loop, to secure it.

CHAIN STITCH

Place the needle into the work, take a stitch to the required length, bring the needle out making sure that the thread is under the needle when making the loop. Insert the needle back into the loop of the previous stitch so that each link of the chain comes from the one before. Suitable for outlines and as a filling stitch.

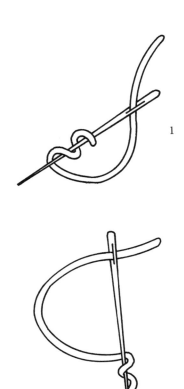

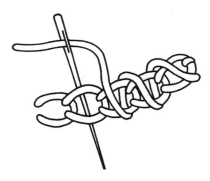

WHIPPED CHAIN STITCH

Complete a row of chain stitches first, then take the needle under each stitch making sure that the fabric is not caught underneath. Suitable for a heavily textured outline stitch.

FRENCH KNOTS

Bring the needle up at the desired position, wind the thread twice or three times around the needle, then insert the point back into the work next to the original place, keeping the thread taut.

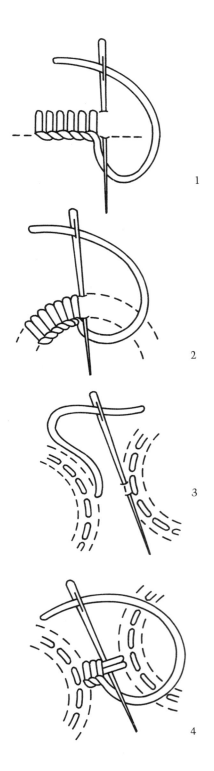

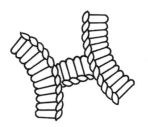

5

BUTTONHOLE STITCH BARS FOR CUTWORK

1 Work buttonhole stitching with the back of the stitches facing the area to be cut out later.

2 When working around a curve, space the stitches evenly, spreading them out slightly.

3 When beginning a bar, come up on one side of the open space, and take a small stitch on the other.

4 Return to the first side and work buttonhole stitches over these foundation threads.

5 A completed buttonhole stitch bar between two rows of buttonhole stitches.

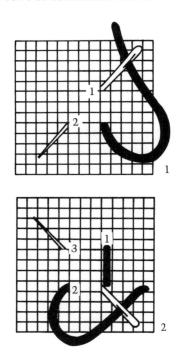

114

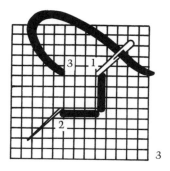

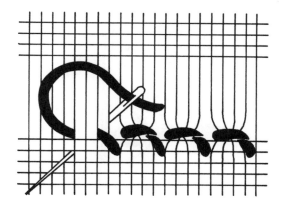

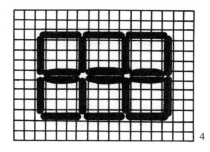

HEM STITCH

The bars are made by catching four (or more or fewer) threads at a time with the needle, then taking a small stitch down two threads into the folded hem at the right-hand side. Work from right to left, keeping the needle below the thread at all times. Be sure not to pull the fabric too tight.

FOUR-SIDED STITCH

This particular pulled-thread stitch is worked in horizontal rows and always from right to left.

1 To begin, come up at the bottom point and go down at 1, coming out at 2.
2 Take the needle down to the left of the last stitch and come out at 3.
3 Then go back in at 1 and out at 2.
4 Finally, take the needle down at 3, and come out four threads further on to begin the next stitch. For reverse four-sided stitch, work on the wrong side of the material so that the reverse side is shown on the front.

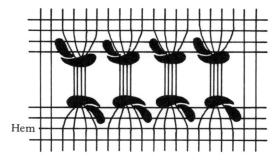

DOUBLE LADDER HEM STITCH

The inner side of the row of drawn threads is worked exactly the same as the hem side, forming a row of bars of several threads pulled tightly together.

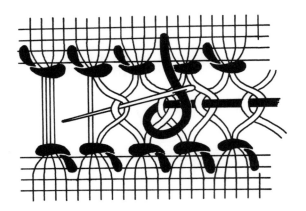

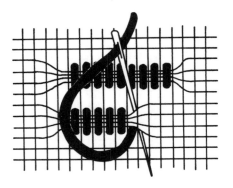

INTERLACED HEM STITCH

After the ladder hem stitch has been completed, work an interlacing thread through the centre of the bars, twisting them from left to right. To work this interlacing, pass the needle over two threads on the right-hand side of the following bar, twist the needle and pass it under the two left-hand threads of the previous group and pull the thread through.

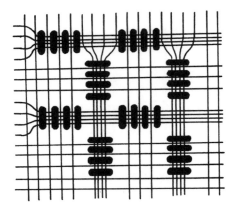

SATIN STITCH AND CHEQUERED SATIN STITCH

Work satin stitch over four or five threads, pulling them tightly so that the space between the rows becomes larger and the bars of stitches are firm. Alternate directions for the chequered satin stitch.

Bibliography

Cronin, L. 1989, *Concise Australian Flora*, Reed Books Pty Ltd, NSW.

de Denne, L. 1979, *Creative Needlecraft*, Octopus Books, London.

Fletcher, M. 1989, *Needlework in Australia*, Oxford University Press, South Melbourne.

Isaacs, J. 1987, *The Gentle Arts*, Lansdowne Press, Willoughby, NSW.

Morcombe, M. 1970, *Australia's Wildflowers*, Summit Books, NSW.

Pascoe, M. 1979, *Blackwork*, Search Press Limited, London.

Petersen, G. & Svennas, E. 1970, *Handbook of Stitches*, B. T. Batsford Limited, London.

Suppliers

Swanland Crafts
PO Box 228
Belmont WA 6104
Tel: (09) 454 4276
This is a mail order firm based in Western Australia which will send greeting card blanks and bookmark blanks anywhere in Australia. They do not have agencies in other states.

Rajmahal
Fosterville Road
Bagshot East VIC 3551
Tel: (054) 48 8551
This firm supplies silk threads by mail order to the public.

Country Patchwork Cottage
10/86 Erindale Road
Balcatta WA 6021
Tel: (09) 345 3550

Helan's Smocking & Patchworks
Shop 3, Barkly Square
53–55 Barkly Street
Mornington VIC 3931
Tel: (059) 75 8076

Rags & Patches
3 Canning Road
Kalamunda WA 6076
Tel: (09) 293 3895

Penbrook Cottage
45 Moulder St
Orange NSW 2800
Tel: (063) 62 0461

Just Patchwork
Shop 5, 70 Princes Hwy
Beaconsfield VIC 3808
Tel: (03) 796 1667

Ribbons & Rainbows
Collier Arcade
Govetts Leap Rd
Blackheath NSW 2785
Tel: (047) 87 7574

Patchwork Supplies
43 Gloucester Street
Highgate Hill QLD 4104
Tel: (07) 844 9391

Five Oaks Australia
Factory 1, 45 Dingley Ave
Dandenong VIC 3175
Tel: (03) 792 0599
This is a potpourri supplier who will supply potpourri and oils throughout Australia.

Potpourri and Sachet Supplies
PO Box 53A
Northcote VIC 3070
Tel: (03) 482 2677
This firm will supply a free mail order service and catalogue throughout Australia and New Zealand.

Acknowledgments

I would like to thank all the people who have helped me in the writing of this book because without their co-operation, I could never have completed it.

DMC Needlecraft, who willingly supplied all the stranded cottons, metallic threads, Aida fabric and linen. All of these DMC products are available through embroidery shops and haberdashery departments of the larger department stores.

My friends · who worked on some of the projects for me, namely Gail Kitchin, Jean Jenkinson, Helen McDonough, Meg Johnson, and also a big thank you to Susan Baker who pieced the quilt cover.

Once again, Hellen Stratton and Shirley Moulds from Kalamunda Art Gallery in Western Australia have done an excellent job with the framing of the pictures.

Mike and Suzanne Hood from The Victorian Photo Company of Kalamunda, Western Australia, for taking a handful of mismatched family photographs and turning them into an interesting collection of sepia-toned portraits.

Jan Kaisler, the Vice-president of the Lutheran Textile Artists Foundation in Adelaide, Mrs Margaret Zweck from Light Pass who generously shared with me the information from her very comprehensive collection of early Lutheran embroidery and Mr Noris Ioannou of Norwood, who was the arts and crafts contributor in the 150th anniversary publication, *The Barossa: A Vision Realised*. Currently Noris is writing an account of Folk Art of the Barossa Valley.

OUR HERITAGE IN CROSS STITCH AND EMBROIDERY
First published in Australasia in 1993 by
Simon & Schuster Australia
20 Barcoo Street, East Roseville NSW 2069

A Paramount Communications Company
Sydney New York London Toronto Tokyo Singapore

© 1993 Vivienne Garforth
© 1993 Photographs Simon & Schuster Australia

Published by Blitz Editions
an imprint of
Bookmart Limited
Registered Number 2372865
Trading as Bookmart Limited
Desford Road
Enderby
Leicester
LE9 5AD

Designed by Anna Warren
Photography by Andrew Elton
Typeset in Australia by Asset Typesetting Pty Ltd
Printed in Hong Kong by South China Printing Co. Ltd